*Tributes*

Shawn is a guy who possesses so many talents, and is so intriguing. He is so mature for his age that he's a breath of fresh air. I've always said the only difference between Kareem Abdul-Jabbar and Shawn Bradley is Bradley is from Castle Dale and Jabbar is from Harlem. He is a great athlete, maybe more of an all-around athlete than most big men his size. And he's a great person. He has a great future in the NBA.

—Frank Layden
President, Utah Jazz

Though . . . he [was] enrolled at Brigham Young University for only one year, Shawn Bradley has had enormous impact for good in our behalf. We are so proud that he is one of our alumni. His basketball skills have brought him the public visibility and therefore the opportunity to do good beyond winning basketball games. But his real contribution to the Church, to BYU, to his family, and to society in general is to be found in the great skill with which he has used that visibility to declare his commitment to gospel-centered principles and values.

I look forward to maintaining a continuing relationship with Shawn, both personally and also on behalf of the university. We are pleased and proud that although he no longer wears our blue and white uniform, everywhere he goes he will be a highly effective goodwill ambassador for BYU and the LDS church.

—Rex E. Lee
President, Brigham Young University

Shawn was an absolute pleasure to coach! He was anxious to learn, a quick study; and did he ever love to have fun. Not only was I Shawn's coach, but my son, Jason, was one of his closest friends and teammates, and so I knew Shawn in our home and in our lives. He offered one of the prayers at Jason's mission farewell, and his spiritual depth is an inspiration to all of us. He is totally respectful, and has a greatness that even he doesn't understand. But, if he remains true to himself, and his God, I have a sense that with his giant frame and giant heart, as well as his remarkable athletic abilities, he will revolutionize the NBA.

—James R. Nelson
Teacher and coach, Emery High School

Shawn Bradley has the greatest skills—passing and shooting—of any seven-foot player who has ever played the game. Wilt, Kareem, Walton— none had the skills he has. Plus, he has an absolutely beautiful attitude toward the team and toward the game. Shawn has some of the greatest potential in basketball ever—not just in Utah, but ever. We may have seen grow up right here the greatest player of our time.

—Jim Yerkovich
Utah all-star coach

Shawn is a great young man who really cares about people and sees how he can be an influence in the lives of others by his commitment to the Church and through his remarkable athletic skills. Even though we will miss Shawn at the Y, I have full confidence that he entered the NBA arena with full integrity. He will be able to make an impact in the lives of people throughout the world that is difficult to measure. Not only will he make a great player, but his missionary zeal and his commitment to excellence has the potential of changing the complexion of the NBA.

—Dale R. McCann
Cougar Club executive director,
Brigham Young University

Shawn was the most visible and highly recruited athlete to ever play at BYU. Shawn has great athletic ability for a man of 7 feet 6 inches. He has a great shooting touch, along with coordination and running ability. Along with his athletic ability, he is an outstanding young man. I will always appreciate the year Shawn spent at the Y, and I wish him every success as he begins his career with Philadelphia and the NBA.

—Roger Reid
Head coach, BYU

The uniqueness of Shawn Bradley is that he is absolutely fun to watch during a basketball game because he brings a certain mystique and excitement to the game. Because of his versatility and toughness, and his spiritual commitment, I personally believe he will be an NBA All-Star in the future.

—Tony Ingle
Assistant coach, BYU

Shawn is one of the best athletes I've ever recruited, or had the opportunity to coach. In my opinion, his future will be very bright in the NBA.

—Charles Bradley
Assistant coach, BYU

He has a chance to be the best big man who ever played. It's not like he's just a big goon. I've never seen a 7-6 guy that well coordinated.

—Jerry Tarkanian
Head coach, UNLV

Bradley blocked all those shots and never changed expression, never did any taunting. They could build a national championship team around him.

—Mike Pollio
Head coach, Eastern Kentucky

Shawn fights you like a guy 5-10. Usually, big guys at that stage are very bland. He's not, he's a warrior. He blocks everything but the Midtown Tunnel. In a few years, God willing he stays healthy, you're going to see a Wooden Award winner.

—Lou Carnesecca
Head coach, St. Johns University

Although one is immediately impressed by Shawn's imposing physical stature, the true measure of this young man is not accomplished simply in terms of feet and inches. I have watched Shawn cultivate qualities of character to equal the rare physical gifts with which he is blessed. Shawn is a winner in every sense of the word, both on and off the court.

—Chuck Tebbs
Coach, Utah all-stars

Shawn is as tall spiritually as he is physically. This has been demonstrated by his willingness to bend his knees to children and to the Savior, in deference to desires of his own, or of worldly importance. I have observed him maintain spiritual equilibrium in the midst of spiraling acclamation.

—Barry N. Norton
Principal, Huntington Junior High

Many people are endowed with superior gifts and talents, but few are able to capitalize on them. Shawn Bradley has done that, and I'm confident that his ability to magnify these gifts and talents will be even more noticeable in the future.

—Glen Tuckett
Athletic director, BYU

As I've watched Bradley, he's got an asset you can't put a price tag on, and that's a good touch around the basket. Sometimes you see a player who is big, but doesn't have any touch. He's an aircraft carrier, a franchise player. His kind doesn't come along very often.

—Jim Spencer
Former Provo High coach

Shawn is the greatest athlete I have ever coached. But more than that, he has always been mature beyond his years—a true leader. He has a sixth sense about people, and about how he can respond to their needs. The tallest men keep their heads bowed, and after all else, that is Shawn Bradley. He was cut out of a different mold, and is the tallest of them all.

—Todd Jeffs
Emery High basketball coach

He stands tall, he walks tall. I felt the strength coming from his hand when he shook my hand, and he wasn't trying to crush it. He's hard-working, he's genuine. Nothing flamboyant.

—Fred Carter
Coach, Philadelphia 76ers

He's Manute Bol with 100 times more athletic ability.

—Jeff Ruland
Assistant coach, Philadelphia 76ers

Now, it's up to you [Sixers fans]. You can enjoy him or you can try to destroy him. Give him a chance. He might just help dig this team out of the rubble.

—Stan Hochman
Philadelphia *Daily News*

Shawn's attitude is not affected by his altitude. He has a tremendous attitude. He is a tremendous example to young people. He is very confident, and has great self-esteem. He is someone to be emulated. He emulates great LDS home life.

—George Curtis
Trainer, BYU

We've had a couple of athletes who have been put through the paces by the media, and Shawn handles himself as well as any of them. The media would ask us about him, then come back after the interview and tell us he was as good as advertised.

—Ralph R. Zobell
Sports information director, BYU

You get a [top-level] center every twenty and a half years; a guy like Bradley, maybe never in the history of a franchise. Philadelphia had Wilt Chamberlain; now it looks like it'll get Bradley. He's the cornerstone, and you put the pieces around him.

—Marty Blake
NBA scout

Shawn is not just a shot-blocker. He has great hands, he can pass, he can score from the outside or on the low box. He makes free throws. He's truly an amazing tall person. I don't think we've ever seen a guy like him in the league. He'll be an impact player with a huge upside.

—Don Nelson
Coach, Golden State Warriors

I think Shawn has a terrific feel for basketball. For a tall player, he is immensely gifted. He plays with a tremendous intensity. . . . He has a number of skills you don't associate with a player his size. Bradley is arguably as good an athlete at that size as we've ever seen. Off the court he's a gentle giant, a people person. Because of his size, it's easy to say he will stand out. But he has that certain something. I don't know how to define it. He relates incredibly well.

—Jimmy Lynam
General manager, Philadelphia 76ers

I added "blocked shots" to our TV stats after watching Shawn's first game as a Cougar. I added the word "class" after watching him meet with fans and Church members. He is warm and friendly off the court, but opponents find him competitive and intense. Shawn will succeed in the NBA, and bring credit to himself, his family, and his church.

—Jay Monsen
KBYU Television sports announcer

He's very, very rough around the edges. But we're going to sand-blast him to the point we have a diamond to show off, kind of like the two on my championship rings from the Detroit Pistons.

—Mike Abdenour
Trainer, Philadelphia 76ers

We have a dinosaur quarry in nearby Cleveland, an area that has produced some of the biggest creatures in the world. With our son, Shawn, we were just keeping in step. We have been looking up to Shawn, a giant in our eyes, since he was in preschool. Even though he is totally normal, he is every parent's wish in a child.

—Reiner and Teresa Bradley
Shawn's Parents

Shawn Bradley is the biggest gamble I've ever taken.

—Harold Katz
Owner, Philadelphia 76ers

I don't know if I'm the biggest ever, but I agree when Harold Katz says I'm the biggest gamble he's ever taken. If I were in his shoes, I'd say the same thing—if I'd had enough guts to take me in the first place.

—Shawn Bradley

STANDING TALL

The
SHAWN
BRADLEY
Story

"Drop in the Bucket"

STANDING TALL

The
SHAWN
BRADLEY
Story

As told to
BRENTON YORGASON

BOOKCRAFT
Salt Lake City, Utah

Library of Congress Catalog Card Number: 93-74223
ISBN 0-88494-912-5

Second Printing, 1994

Printed in the United States of America

To my mom and dad, Teresa and Reiner Bradley. All that I am, or hope to become, I owe to them. In my mind, they're the world's greatest parents.

 *Contents*

Author's Note

When Shawn first asked me to help him write his life story, I was deeply honored. I had followed his high school and college careers, had watched from afar as moments from his mission in Australia were shared through the media, and had been impressed with the character and integrity he exhibited. Even so, at that early hour I had no idea of the impact that this gentle, persuasive giant would have on my life.

On 23 September 1989, as Shawn was just beginning his senior year at Emery High School, the LDS-owned *Church News* published an article titled "His Character Is As Big As He Is." When I read this article, I couldn't help considering my own seven sons, one of whom was born just two days before Shawn was and whose "Drop in the Bucket" sketch introduces this book. I silently hoped that each of my sons, like Shawn, was becoming a man of true character. In that article, Mike Cannon wrote, "Bradley, a 17-year-old senior and standout basketball star at Emery High School in rural Castle Dale, Utah, re-writes the definition of 'walking tall.'"

It seemed therefore appropriate to title Shawn's book *Standing Tall*. While Shawn has had a fairly normal childhood, making the common mistakes of youth, still he has had a daily quest not only to stand tall before his Maker but also to lift others to their full height. After all else is said about Shawn, this trait is what makes his life worth knowing.

Brenton G. Yorgason

 *Foreword*

As Shawn's parents, we would like to jointly express our great joy and satisfaction in rearing him. Never in our wildest dreams did we anticipate the course his life would take—though dream we did, along with all of those whose lives Shawn touched. There was always a direction he was heading, a goal he had in front of him, a dream he was following, and as his parents we felt it our duty to reinforce his direction and do all we could to not interfere with his progress.

As Shawn grew, we would match his age with the normal curve on a pediatric growth chart; he would be not only over the 100th percentile but usually "off the chart." We found ourselves having to step back and observe Shawn with his friends, which made us more aware of how much older we may have been treating him. This was also reflected in how others treated Shawn, and it had a profound influence in why he seemed to mature more quickly.

In Shawn's youth, his love of sports opened many doors for baseball and basketball competition; because of his stature, we always had to carry a certified copy of his birth certificate so that he would be permitted to play. His age was frequently questioned as he literally stood head and shoulders—and sometimes chest—above his disbelieving opponents.

Shawn has always been a good kid—impulsively competitive, gentle with children, hardworking, goal oriented, and mischievously playful. He rarely did anything halfheartedly. In fact, he would usually push things right to the edge, as if to test his limits—or occasionally the limits of others. For example, his idea of snow skiing was to point the skis straight down the slope and just go for it. A dunk was not good enough unless there was a chance the backboard would break—which happened twice that we know of. The thrill of riding a three-wheeler was not complete unless he could get it airborne. Being up to bat was not a total success unless the ball sailed over the fence.

Thank goodness in some ways Shawn has come down to earth, because it is this nature that causes parents of all such children to get gray hair, wrinkles, and heart attacks. But it is also this nature that makes Shawn who he is today. This nature was the driving force on his mission, where he dedicated his all to the service of his God. And Shawn returned home rewarded for his diligence by having served well and honorably and by having left a noticeable mark for the Church on the continent of Australia. It is this—his love for his Church—that gives us, his parents, the greatest joy. This alone will always nurture and sustain him in whatever life has in store for him.

One of the most difficult questions to answer is, How did we rear such a one as Shawn? We have no magical answer. It was no more, yet no less, than being at his side whenever he needed us, and many times when he thought he didn't. Suffice it to say, we tried to always be there for his games, his adventures, his failures and successes, his ebbs and his tides. And so shall we continue, because there is no greater joy for parents than to be at the side of their child when that child is doing his very best at whatever it may be that he's doing. There is an inner peace, a profound satisfaction, and an inward exhilaration to know we may have had a part in Shawn's success. And thus we will continue—to be at his side and at the side of our other three children—as they progress through life. It will be our hope and prayer that as interested yet unobtrusive spectators we will be always available when ordeals require embrace and love from us.

Our greatest joy as Shawn's parents has been to watch the

development of his character, his love for people and for his religion. He has touched the lives of many, but none more than us, his parents. Shawn has many ardent supporters, but again, none more than us, his parents. We pray he will always remain an influence of good and integrity to all those whose lives touch his.

Reiner and Teresa Bradley

 *Preface*

It feels strange writing a book, especially one about myself when I am not yet twenty-two years old! But, as someone who has been blessed with extra long limbs and a tremendous love for basketball and life, it just feels like the thing to do.

Before reading this book, you need to know that I am proud to be a member of The Church of Jesus Christ of Latter-day Saints, a people sometimes known as Mormons. I have a deep respect for people of all faiths, and especially welcome those of you of other religions into the pages of my life. As my story unfolds, I will share with you my own quest for truth and explain how my values have afforded me the blessings I now enjoy.

I am asked so many questions about myself, and why I do the things I do, that I want to answer these questions. So now, as I enter the world of professional basketball, allow me to share with you my ups and downs, and let you know how certain events and decisions have brought me to this point.

Even though I certainly have my share of weaknesses, I want all of you, from age nine to ninety, to know that above all I am a Christian. I have a sure knowledge that Jesus of Nazareth is the Savior of the world and that our lives will be enriched as we make a total commitment to living as he taught.

And so, as you begin chapter 1, know that I am a very happy person who simply wants to stand as tall as my Heavenly Father would have me stand. Many people have jokingly said that I live with my head in the clouds, while I just consider myself a little closer to heaven. But seriously, I hope that you will enjoy my "journey of preparation" and that you will feel the spirit in which I am sharing my life with you.

Sincerely,

Shawn

1

Our First State Championship

Perspiration beaded on my forehead as I glanced up at the clock in the locker room. Five minutes till game time! We had completed our warm-ups, and now, as I wiped my face with a towel, I glanced around the room at my teammates. I smiled inwardly, as I could sense that they were as nervous as I was.

"All right, guys, let's go over our game plan one last time...." Coach Todd Jeffs was speaking. As always, he had his clipboard in his hands and was prepared. Although I was just a junior and had only played for him the past two years, I had already learned much at his hands. And he had not just taught me about basketball, either, although that was always on his mind. He had also taught me about life and about how I should carry myself as a role model for those younger than me.

"We've just got a few minutes," he continued, interrupting my thoughts. "But before I give you my last instructions, let me tell you that regardless of the outcome of our game with Richfield, in my book each one of you is a true champion. There isn't one of you I wouldn't love to have as my own son."

That was Coach Jeffs, all right—always building us up as individuals, not just as athletes.

"... But I honestly believe we can take the state championship trophy back to Castle Dale with us, if we each do our part."

I don't recall the last words he spoke—at that instant I ran into the adjoining room and threw up. My nerves were a total mess, but after losing my lunch I felt somewhat better.

A few minutes later, as we ran onto the court, the crowd was in sheer pandemonium, with each school trying to out-yell the other. One side of the stands was filled with Richfield Wildcat fans, and the other was jammed with Emery Spartans. It was electrifying, that's for sure.

Our guards were Todd Huntington and Steve Gordon, and our forwards were Ryan Stilson and Lynn Tuttle. The five of us had evolved into a cohesive unit, and I was glad to be on the floor with them.

Before the game began, I shook hands with my friend Ryan Cuff, the 6'4" star of Richfield's team. Ryan and I had played together in summer tournaments over the years, and I knew how much winning the state championship meant to him. After all, his team had won it the year before, when he was only a sophomore—and he was voted Most Valuable Player of the tournament. He was such a great competitor and athlete, and I knew one of us would be in ecstasy in about an hour and a half, while the other would be in total depression. I also knew, as we stood there, that our feelings toward each other were much different than our respective communities thought. Richfield fans thought I was something like a child of the devil, and Emery fans thought Ryan was. But neither he nor I bought into that. Instead, we respected each other for having the same values and for trying to honor those values both on and off the court. But for now, we were combatants, locked in a war that would leave only one of us victorious.

As the game began, each team scored in spurts, one going up a few points and then the other team coming back and doing the same. Neither of us could gain the advantage, and it was obvious to me that the game would go right down to the wire.

With about thirty seconds left to play, the game was tied at 73. We had the ball and called time-out. Coach Jeffs mapped out a play where the other four would work the ball around the perimeter and then feed it in to me for the final winning shot. The play worked like magic—that is, until the ball came toward me. Somehow it was deflected, and all of a sudden players were diving all over the court, scooting the ball first into back-court, then back again to us. But we couldn't control it, and it just squirted around like it had a mind of its own.

Finally, with just one second to go, Ryan Cuff got the ball for Richfield. He was standing about three feet behind their three-point line and jumped to shoot—an average-length shot for him. But as he went into the air, the buzzer went off, ending the game. So, without shooting, he came back down with the ball, and we went to our respective benches to prepare for overtime. I was totally relieved, because I knew that if Ryan had gotten his shot off, he would have made it. He is just that kind of a money player.

As I grabbed a towel and a drink, I thought of how this game was even more exciting than the one the week before, at the regional play-offs. I was so tired that I could hardly catch my breath, and yet strangely I felt like I had more energy than I knew what to do with.

The overtime period finally began, and we quickly went up by eight points. But Ryan was a pure winner, and before we knew what had happened, he had hit two consecutive three-pointers. Then the game went crazy. First I would hit a basket, and our fans would scream; then he would, and the other side of the arena would erupt. I felt like I was almost playing in a trance, it was so eery.

Finally, again with thirty seconds left, we found ourselves with the ball and the score tied. It was a repeat of regulation play, only in this time-out, Coach gave us a different play. I was excited because again it involved lobbing the ball in to me. I was supposed to then turn, put it softly in the basket, and win the game.

Everything went like clockwork. The ball came in bounds, then was lofted over the head of my opponent, Troy Brown, into my hands. I simply turned, jumped into the air, and . . . and then I heard a whistle blow. In a way I was relieved, since I was sure the ref had whistled Troy for the foul. I knew we had bumped each other a little bit, but I didn't think it was enough for the whistle to be blown.

Thinking that I had been fouled, I started walking over to the free throw line. I knew it would either be a two-shot foul or a one-and-one. I started concentrating on hitting the foul shot when I saw the ref out of the corner of my eye. He pointed in my direction, but since Troy was standing next to me, I thought he was pointing at him.

The next thing I knew, the ref ran over to the scorer's table and shouted, "Number forty-five—pushing off!" He then pointed in the direction of the other basket. Needless to say, I was dumbfounded. Of all the fouls that had been called on me, this was certainly the worst. There was no way I had fouled my man. No way.

Totally disgusted and stunned, I walked with my teammates to the other end of the court and lined up for the foul shots. I decided to keep my cool, but at that moment I looked into the stands and saw tempers flare. My dad came out of his seat; our principal, Brent Arnold, who was also our stake president, came out of his; and Coach Jeffs flipped his lid! It was a totally outrageous call, and at a time that would determine the state championship. It was unbelievable! I truly thought that ref was a dead man.

Within seconds, however, tempers calmed, and Troy walked up to the line to shoot one-and-one. All I could think of was how he could be a hero forever if he made the shots. The word was that he had stayed in the Centrum shooting foul shots until 10:30 the night before, and so he had paid his dues to put them in.

As Troy was bouncing the ball in preparation to shoot, I glanced over to the ref who had made the call. He was standing next to me, and so I softly said, "You kind of missed that one, didn't you, ref?" He admitted that he in fact had, and apologized to me. That was when I lost it emotionally. I didn't want to get a technical, though, so I just shook my head in disgust. No way should we lose the state championship on a bad call like that.

Finally Troy poised himself and let the ball fly. I boxed out, ready to rebound, but the ball hit nothing but the bottom of the net. That meant we were down by one point with just six seconds left in overtime. Rather than let him shoot the second shot, we called a time-out and walked over to our bench. We were all stunned beyond belief, and our side of the arena was deathly silent. Richfield's fans, on the other hand, were acting like they had just won the war of the worlds!

When we sat down, Coach Jeffs knelt in front of us, and

said, "Guys, I don't know what to say. You've worked your hearts out all year long, and you deserve to win. Now, listen. If he misses his second foul shot, get the ball down the court and take the best shot you can. If he makes it, do the same thing. If we make a three-pointer, we'll either win by one or by two. If we make a two-pointer, we'll either win by one, or tie, and then go into a second overtime. I don't care what you do, just win!"

All I could think of when I went back onto the court was that we didn't have a set play. What we *did* have was five teammates who knew how to win. Somehow I knew we could do it, if we just kept our cool.

Richfield's center then took the ball, let it fly—swish. They were now ahead by two, 83-81, and our challenge was ahead of us. Running back down the floor, I saw that Ryan Stilson was having a hard time getting the ball in bounds. Cody, our point guard, was being worn like a glove, and Ryan couldn't get it to him. He then saw Steven Gordon, our second guard, and successfully threw the ball in to him.

Steve dribbled behind his back between two players and approached the half-court stripe. Those moves took three seconds off the clock. Sensing that he had no more time to dribble, Steve quickly cocked his arm and let the ball fly. He was forty-five feet from the basket, and even though I was open under the basket, he didn't see me. Instead, I could see that he was shooting. In a time span that seemed like an eternity, I poised myself for a rebound, knowing the ball was going to bounce hard off the rim or backboard. But as the ball came down over my shoulder, I suddenly *knew* that it was going in the basket.

Just as the buzzer sounded and the light flashed a bright red, the ball hit the backboard, passed through the net, and hit the floor! I looked at the ball, then at the scoreboard, and then back at the ref to see if he was going to count it. He did—the final score was 84-83! We had won our first-ever state championship, and in disbelief I ran over, grabbed Steve, and fell to the ground. Before I knew what was happening, the team, the cheerleaders, and the rest of the world had jumped on top of me, nearly crushing me to death! It was the most awesome, terrifying moment of my life!

When everyone finally got off me, I worked my way to my feet, and walked over to shake hands with the Richfield players. They were in total shock, as they realized that against all odds the final seconds had taken the victory away from them. Two times in as many weeks we had beaten them—first at region, and now at state. And to think that they were the two-time defending state champions!

Later in the evening, after we had showered and dressed, I was asked to meet with the press. In responding to their questions, one reporter asked what I was thinking when Steve put up his forty-five-foot game winner. Smiling, I simply said, "I had a prayer, and it was answered in the affirmative." Everyone laughed, but in my heart, I didn't think I was far off. I don't know that God really cared who won the game, but I do think he likes to see people do their best.

That night we returned to our motel, where we celebrated into the early morning hours. We finally got a couple of hours sleep, then celebrated again over breakfast before we began to form a bus-and-car caravan back to Castle Dale. Most of our fans had also stayed for the night, wanting to take part in the horn-honking trip home.

Coach Jeffs and I were the last to climb up into the bus for our return trip to Castle Dale. Always there had been reporters, and this morning was no different. In its twenty-six-year history, this was the first time the Spartans had claimed a state championship trophy. But we had earned it—the players, the coaches, and the seven small communities that fed into Emery High. It was a team and county victory, to be sure. But for me, after spending the year under the spotlight, the feelings were quite personal. I knew that I had done my best with what I had been given and that I had made a contribution to our community, as well as to our team. Although I had scored 37 points and pulled down 12 rebounds, the stat that I was most proud of was the final score, 84-83, in favor of Emery. The feeling was awesome!

Moments later, after finishing the last of an apple, I pulled the bill of my hat down over my eyes and took a deep breath. Then, while listening to the smooth, whining sound of the engine, I closed my eyes and let the air escape slowly from my lungs. Never in all the world, I considered, had anyone been more blessed than me. Not only had I proven myself to be a champion, but I was surrounded by the greatest family and friends a guy could ask for. With a smile spreading slowly across my face, I quietly fell asleep.

Before I knew what was happening, we were greeted at the Emery County line by a police escort, and the honking was nonstop from there into Castle Dale. As we passed through every town, sirens blared and people lined the streets, cheering their returning champions. I was awfully tired, but each town brought a new set of emotions, and before long, we arrived at our high school, where we gathered and formally celebrated in true Emery High Spartan style.

2

Early Footprints

Like all families, my ancestors left a colorful trail. They were born throughout the world, moved across continents and mountains, married into other families, and watched their posterity grow. While I would selfishly like to lay out my entire family tree, for the purposes of this book I will limit my tellings to my father and mother's namesake lines. Their stories are miraculous in their own right and provide a bloodline of rugged tenacity that leaves no doubt in my mind about who I am.

My Father's Ancestors

On 20 June 1837, Queen Victoria ascended to the throne in England. Thirty-three days later, an event transpired that would forever change the course of many of her subjects. On that day, the first sermon by missionaries of the Mormon faith was preached on England's soil. Among the first to embrace the gospel of Jesus Christ as taught by these and successive missionaries was my third great-grandfather, John Bradley. At the time, he and his father, Isaac Bradney (notice the different last name), were working in the coal mines near the township of Pontesbury.

Sometime in the mid-1840s, John and his wife, Mary, moved with their three daughters to Monmouthshire, an area that was claimed by both England and Wales. They obviously felt they were upgrading their standard of living by making this move, since John was able to escape the mines and begin to work at the iron works plant. They also became proprietors of a "public house," more commonly called a pub, that they named The Lamb and Flag.

While living and working at their pub, they hosted missionaries, were baptized members of the Church, and even held meetings in a large room on the upper floor. Here they lived frugally, saving their extra shillings, until at last, in 1862, they sailed from Liverpool on board the *John J. Boyd*. Before many weeks passed, they arrived in New York, then journeyed to Florence, Nebraska. From that point, they joined a wagon train that allowed them to trek the fifteen hundred miles across the plains. At last, as the leaves of autumn began to change their color, John and Mary and their children arrived in the valley of the Great Salt Lake, where they began a new life on the western frontier. They were asked by Brigham Young to travel northeast and settle in the small farming hamlet of Hyrum, Utah.

The generations passed, and in 1926 my dad's father, Vincent Eli Bradley, was born in Malad, Idaho, after the family had left Hyrum. Vince, or "Opa" as we called him (which is the German expression for Grandpa), grew up on the family farm there and lived the strenuous life on the farm without too many complaints. From what I understand, though, he was excited to leave the farm and attend Westminster College in Salt Lake City.

I should mention here that Great-grandpa Iver Bradley did not live his life as an active member of the LDS faith. My great-grandmother, Bobbie Routh, was a Southern Baptist, and so basically Opa grew up in that environment. The family didn't practice the Mormon faith, but they did maintain strong Christian values in their home. They were of high moral stature, regularly read from the scriptures, had family and personal prayers, and believed that Christ was in fact the Savior of the world.

Iver died of a heart attack when Opa was just ten years old.

This made things difficult for their family, but he grew strong and committed to his values and felt that he could make a valid contribution in his chosen field of teaching school.

After receiving his associate degree in elementary education from Westminster, Opa was drafted into the army. With World War II being waged in the European and Pacific arenas, Opa soon found himself stationed in the Philippines. Thank goodness he survived, and following the war, he was transferred to Germany to assist in the postwar Allied Occupation efforts. Here he met Friedl Franziska Guerdan, a beautiful brunette who immediately captured his heart. They were wed 3 September 1948. Later that fall, Opa returned to civilian life in Salt Lake City, Utah, with his war bride at his side.

As Opa began his career of teaching school, Oma (the German expression for Grandma) gave birth to their eldest son and my father, Reiner Paul Bradley. He was born 15 July 1949 in Salt Lake City, the first of four children. After Dad's birth, the small family moved from place to place, even spending four years, from when he was eight years old until he was twelve, in Germany. For the first two years in the country, he attended a German primer school where Opa taught. Then, when Opa was given a new teaching contract with the American military schools, Dad transferred to the base schools for the final two years.

At age ten, Dad was thought to be advanced enough in his learning to be given a double grade promotion. This automatically put him in with peers a year older than him, but he fit right in and continued to work at the top level of his grade.

While attending the German elementary school, Dad became a member of a German boys choir. When he first heard the choir performing, he thought he was hearing a bunch of girls. Although his mother assured him that they were all boys, he still didn't quite believe her until he was invited to join and to sing soprano with the rest of the "girls." At that time, he began to really enjoy the status of belonging to this elite group.

After four years in Germany, Dad and his family moved back to the States, settling in Nevada—first in Lovelock for a year, then Reno, and finally nearby Sparks. Opa taught at Reno High School as Dad and his brothers and sister grew.

Dad loved being involved in activities. He became an Eagle Scout within the Methodist-church-sponsored organization and loved the challenge that Scouting brought to his life. He especially enjoyed competing against the Mormon-sponsored Scout troops at the annual summer camps. He had no earthly idea that his ancestry had been Mormon, since his father had never mentioned it to him, so Scouting was the only involvement he had with the Church while he was growing up.

Dad was also involved in student government at Sparks High School; at one time he was even named Lieutenant Governor for the Day for the state of Nevada. The following year he was named as Governor for the Day and had exciting write-ups in the paper for this. He still claims that he nearly took over the government by the time the sun set that evening.

Although Dad loved athletics, he didn't have a lot of opportunity to play basketball in high school. But at 6'7" and with promising potential, the coach granted him a two-year tuition waiver to play on the junior varsity team for the University of Nevada at Reno. He also left high school with several academic scholarships. These were helpful, and because he also joined the Army ROTC, his college life was filled to the brim.

After two years of college, Dad transferred to the University of Utah, in Salt Lake City. He knew of their medical program, and since he wanted to become a physician, he felt that being on a campus with a medical school would enhance his possibility of being accepted. And so he enrolled, majoring in pre-med and biology and working as an orderly in the hospital on campus. He thought of trying out for the basketball team, but because he felt his skills were not quite on that level and his studies were so demanding, he resigned himself to believe that his playing days were over. Little did he know of the workouts I would give him in the years to come!

During this time, Dad again enrolled as a cadet in the Army ROTC program and partially financed his education in this way. He knew he would have a commitment to serve following his graduation, but this seemed adventurous to him, so he excitedly pursued it.

While working as an orderly at the University of Utah Medical Center, Dad's heart felt the emptiness of not being in love. He dated lots of cute girls, but none of them seemed to capture his fancy. He also spent a lot of time skiing during the winter, hoping that his athletic prowess would attract some beautiful young lady. While thinking of whom he might marry, Dad often recalled his father's words of caution before he left for Utah. "You stay away from those Mormon girls," Opa had counseled. "They're beautiful, and they'll gettcha if you're not careful." Little did my dad appreciate the prophetic nature of his father's words.

But that's getting ahead of the story. Perhaps it would now be good to again go back in time to Europe and watch the odyssey unfold that would allow me to come into the world.

My Mother's Ancestors

My third great-grandfather on my mother's side was Lars Olsen Wilberg. He was born in 1815 in Tolten, Norway. He married Caroline Smith Winger, from Oslo, and together they became the parents of seven children. Their fifth child, Carl, was born in 1864 in Moss, Norway. At the time of Carl's birth, his father was a very successful businessman. He owned a large vineyard, as well as a brickyard, and because he owned his own fleet of ships, his bricks were shipped all over the world.

It is unfortunate that this great man died at the early age of fifty-nine, leaving his widow to rear their children and to live without a companion for the final thirty-five years of her life. Caroline's years of being a widow were anything but dull, though, as she and her children joined the Mormon church five months after her husband's death. Both Caroline and Lars had been friends to the Mormon missionaries while he was still alive and had always welcomed them into their home. In fact, Lars had been very generous to the Church, donating money and materials regularly.

At the time of the family's conversion, Caroline sold all of her properties at a value far less than they were worth and migrated with her children to Utah. As my father's ancestors had done, they crossed the plains, but Caroline's family did so in the relative comfort of a train, since the transcontinental railroad had been completed by this time. My great-great-grandfather Carl celebrated his tenth birthday while crossing from east to west and was delighted when his mother settled their family in Ephraim, Sanpete County. Actually, Brigham

Young had asked all of the Scandinavian immigrants to settle in Sanpete County, as he thought their common roots would help them make the adjustment to frontier life. Sanpete folklore remembers that he had another reason for sending them there—his frustration with their languages. In fact, so firm was he in his resolve to understand them that he directed them to speak only English when conversing one with another. I don't know if that plan worked, but my great-grandfather *did* learn to speak English, so I guess "all's well that ends well."

As Carl grew to manhood, he fell in love with Matilda Johnson, and they were wed in 1883. A year later Carl, his wife, and their baby daughter moved in their covered wagon to Provo, where Carl attended the Brigham Young Academy in order to become a schoolteacher. The academy, which later became Brigham Young University, had been founded by President Young in 1875, only eight years before Carl first enrolled there. I'm sure Carl was jumping for joy in the spirit world when 107 years later I also made the same trek north, only this time in my newly painted GMC pickup, to enroll at the same institution.

But to continue. Following his graduation from the academy, Carl received a contract to teach over the mountain from his native Ephraim in the frontier community of Castle Dale, so he and Matilda moved there and he commenced his new profession. His schoolhouse was actually a one-room log cabin, with long wooden slabs for benches. The room was heated by a fireplace in one end and was also used as a place for town meetings and dances.

While Carl taught here, he and Matilda's family continued to grow. Before long, my great-grandfather Warren was born on 12 January 1901. He was the last of eight children and was born in their small home in Castle Dale.

While the family continued to grow, so did Carl's business interests. Before long, he became county clerk and thus arbitrated land disputes and helped establish county boundaries. His knowledge and integrity were unquestioned; because of this, the General Land Office in Salt Lake City would accept his word for whatever boundaries had to be met.

While in office, Carl platted the original boundaries for the counties surrounding Castle Dale. He also designated the boundary line between Carbon and Emery counties. He half-jokingly said that he made the line as far north as he reasonably dared, but later wished he had gone a few miles farther north to include the rich coal mines that are located in Carbon County.

Carl also became deputy sheriff and built a two-story drugstore, using part of it as a doctor's office, where he became handy as a lay doctor, diagnosing and treating ailments and setting broken bones. He also built a sawmill, and then began his lifelong dream of owning a ranch. By 1896, he had a large ranch of shorthorn Durham cattle, along with about 750 head of Angora goats.

But things turned sour for Carl at this time, and before he could recover, he had lost everything. He had given so much credit to people that when they couldn't pay, he had no choice but to close his store down. He even lost his own home, and had to nest without permission in a small vacant shack. The year was 1908. When the owner of the shack found that a family was living there, he rode up on his horse and called, "Hey, what are you doing in my house?" Carl answered back, "I'm not trying to take your property, but I've just gone broke in town. I had no other place to go. I'll get out if you say so, but if you don't need this shack right now, I'd like to stay here until I can find something."

Luckily for Carl, the rancher gave his permission, and so the family lived there until they could acquire land on their own and again return to the cattle business. Before long, Carl had "risen from the financial ashes" and had begun to work his 3,000 acres of rangeland surrounding his new home, as well as 550 acres of fine meadow range at the head of Joe's Valley in the mountain meadows west of town.

Perhaps the most widely acclaimed part of Carl's dream on his ranch was the Wilberg Resort that he built to entertain the peoples of the region. Using its renowned dance floor and the regular big-band dances that were staged, the resort became much more. As a family attraction, there was the swimming pool, the carnival rides for adults and youth, and the large, long fox pens. All that's left now are the ruins, but my grandpa says that folks used to come from all over the state to enjoy the festivities there.

Let me just mention that west of this resort, in the mountains, lies the infamous Wilberg Coal Mine. Named after my great-grandfather, who established it, this mine caught fire on 19 December 1984, killing twenty-six men and one woman who were working inside the mine. It was a tragic disaster, and one that drew somber attention to our area for several years thereafter. Although we didn't have any relatives who died in the fire, many of our family's close friends were killed, and I remember how devastating it was to our community. I was just twelve when this happened, but I surely remember the trauma of it. Our family could see the smoke billowing out of the canyon from our living room window, and it was awful.

Getting back to the story, Carl died in 1951 at the age of eighty-six. He was one of the most prosperous men in the valley and was survived by his seven children, thirty-three grandchildren, and forty-nine great-grandchildren. During his later years, his son and my great-grandfather, Warren, ran the farm for him. But that's getting ahead of the story again. Let me back up a bit.

Grandpa Wayne's Birth

My great-grandfather Warren married Lila Rowley 23 August 1921 in the Manti LDS temple. Living on the ranch, they were able to bear five children. Wayne Ray, my grandfather, was the third to be born, on 15 January 1926. He has always told me that he was born on the kitchen table, assisted by Dr. Hill, Grandma Rowley, the midwife, and the Lord.

Grandpa Wilberg married my grandmother Mary Elaine Cox on 16 September 1949, also in the Manti Temple. Moving into a small home they had purchased in Castle Dale, Grandpa resumed his job of driving a truck. He owned his own truck and jobbed himself out, hauling coal for the LDS church and American Fuel. He also worked a second job, as almost everyone else did, assisting his father on the ranch. He did this until his truck wore out. Because he didn't have money for a new one, and since his dad was getting too old to run the ranch by himself, he went to work as a full-time farmer and rancher. He never did know which he did, farm or ranch, so he finally settled on the fact that he did both! Am I ever glad that this became his profession, because I was able to grow up on that same ranch, working at his side and learning everything he did.

I just hope that when I have kids, they'll have the same opportunity. It was awesome!

Mom's Entry into the World

Two years after my grandparents' marriage, they gave birth to my mother, Teresa, 12 May 1951. Grandpa took my grandmother to Price for the delivery, and Mom was born at the Price Hospital. She was the first of four girls, with my grandparents having no sons. I think this is why Grandpa unofficially adopted me, his oldest grandson, as his son to help him on the ranch.

Growing up in Castle Dale, Mom was very involved in Church and school activities, working out on the farm, feeding cattle, and especially driving tractor for the hay haulers during the harvesting of the three hay crops.

Mom was great in athletics and played Church and county softball, pitching and playing first base. To practice, she painted a red mark on the side of her garage and pitched to that mark every day. She had only one ball, so she made sure she hit that red mark, since she knew with each throw she had to walk down and pick up the ball. Her work ethic paid off, though, when her team was able to win the stake championship. She was fourteen years old at the time.

Perhaps this would be a good place to mention that twelve years later, when Mom played for the newly formed women's county softball league, she became creative in finding a practice field for her team. At that time, she asked her dad if the two of them could build a ball diamond on the ranch. He was quick to comply, and before long, they had leveled the ground and built a backstop with wire and pipe that he had on the ranch.

Looking back on it, and after seeing Kevin Costner's movie, Mom says it was Castle Dale's own version of *Field of Dreams*. It was really a "build it and they will come" sort of experience. The only difference was that instead of corn surrounding the ball field, alfalfa and cattle did, and there never was any mingling with those who had passed on.

Mom also played basketball, volleyball, soccer, and track in P.E. class and became quite an accomplished athlete. Her prowess was not without the occasional mishap, however. For instance, one day during a meet, she hit her arm on the high-jump bar, breaking the arm badly. I'll give her a good 50 percent credit for instilling a love of athletics within me. She's still something else on the smart end of a ball!

The Fall of 1969—Mom Meets Dad, and Hearts Melt

Following high school graduation, Mom went to Salt Lake City and lived in the dorms as she attended LDS Business College. While attending school with her, her girlfriend from home, Jolene Jensen, broke her leg while jumping off a diving board. As Jolene convalesced in the University of Utah Medical Center, Mom and her other roommates came to visit her. While they were standing around her bed, a tall, handsome, pleasant young orderly named Reiner Paul Bradley came into the room to bring Jolene a pitcher of water. According to common family folklore, when their eyes met, they were both smitten. Not only was Mom gorgeous, with what Dad described as a very sexy voice, but she was also six feet tall. Because Dad had grown to 6'8", he began an earnest pursuit. Mom was also totally taken with how handsome Dad was, and she was happy that she had tinted her hair a popular platinum blonde, so that he noticed her.

Unwittingly, while Dad was in the room, Mom gave Jolene her phone number to call her if need be. Well, Dad was listening, and being quick on the uptake, he memorized the number. I can imagine Mom's surprise when, later that night, Dad called her up and asked her on a date! She had no idea he was interested in her, but she soon learned! They dated steadily throughout the winter, and before long they hiked up to the block U on the hill overlooking campus, where Dad first told Mom that he loved her. He really was the adventurous sort.

The next April, while Mom was showing Dad off to the family in Castle Dale, the fireworks really began. She wanted to show him Joe's Valley, so they drove up the canyon and onto Grandpa's grazing land. Here Dad caught the spirit of things and asked Mom to marry him. They say that their hearts were all aflutter, she accepted, and they drove off the mountain planning a Christmas wedding.

Not long after that, Dad had to do some active military duty in Ft. Belvoir, Virginia, and he was so lonely that he sent Mom a telegram directing her to plan for an October wedding instead. He must have sensed that this would likely be the only time he could give her directions, so he went all out—and nearly sent my Grandma Wilberg into a coronary.

Thus it was that in 1970, following a thirteen-month courtship, Mom and Dad tied the knot in the local LDS chapel in Castle Dale. Mom had turned nineteen by this time, and Dad was a very mature twenty-one. I think I was up in heaven praying that they would hurry up and get married so I could be born. But they took their sweet time about it, and as a result, I'm a year younger than perhaps I could be. But I'm not complaining, because I figure that maybe the Lord gave me a few extra inches as compensation for having to wait so long.

As I mentioned, because Great-Grandpa Iver Bradley was not active in the Church, he didn't follow through with having Opa baptized. As a result, Dad had grown up as a Christian but had attended various Protestant churches. It was very difficult for Mom to marry him outside the temple because she believed strongly that an eternal marriage was the only type of marriage worth entering into. But she also loved him deeply and had the faith that if she lived worthily, one day he would gain a testimony of the truthfulness of the restored gospel and want to become a member of the Church. She also felt that once the restored gospel of Jesus Christ was explained to him properly, he couldn't deny the truthfulness of it.

Mom's uncle, Bill Brotherson, from the Uintah Basin, was a stake patriarch in the Church. As such, he lived very close to the Spirit and discerned what lay in store for people when conferring patriarchal blessings on them. When he arrived at the wedding, he was introduced to Dad; he then went into the house and told my Grandmother Elaine that she didn't have to worry, for one day Dad would embrace the gospel in its fulness.

So, Mom and Dad began their lives together, living first in Georgia for two months while Dad completed his airborne training at Fort Benning. They then moved to Germany for three years, to the town of Zweibruecken, where great experiences were in store. One day soon afterward, they answered their door, only to find one of Mom's friends from home standing there.

She invited Mom and Dad to church the next Sunday, and this set a precedent of Church activity for them that would never end.

A Future Giant Is Born

While living in Zweibruecken, Mom became "great with child." After a long nine months, when she was about to give up, she and Dad drove thirty miles in their 1970 red Volkswagen, and she entered the Landstuhl Army Hospital to give birth to her first child. The date was 22 March 1972. Little did they know, as I made my entry into the world, the price they would pay in rearing me! But my birth only cost them eight dollars, so any future costs would be to compensate for such an inexpensive entry into the world.

I was born a true American-German to a father who spoke fluent German *and* English, and to a mother who spoke English, as well as her uniquely native Emery County ranch jargon. I was a normal twenty inches long, I weighed nine pounds fourteen ounces, and other than a little blonde fuzz, I was bald.

I drank and ate everything that was put in front of me. Also, I slept well because my folks were always traveling, enjoying the sites of Europe, and I would fall asleep at the purring of the VW engine. Mom tells me that whenever the engine would stop, I would awaken and want to run everywhere. I actually began walking at nine months.

As a year-old toddler in Germany, and then later back in the United States, I evoked the sympathy of quite a few people. Mom has told me that a few folks came up to her and expressed their sympathy for my seeming lack of coordination in walking. One lady came up to her at church and said, "I'm sorry for your son, for his handicap." She thought I was a handicapped three-year-old, when in reality I was just a really huge one-year-old.

At one year, I had grown immensely and measured in at thirty-six inches in height, weighing twenty-seven pounds. I don't know if it was Mom's German cooking or what, but I loved food, and it was beginning to show.

Great Changes

Not long after this, in November of 1973, Dad found his stint in the army coming to an end. Because of this, Mom flew with me back to Utah to attend my Aunt Sandra's wedding and to then live on the ranch until Dad returned to continue his schooling. I think she was excited to show me off, since I was such a cute little kid, and she was the first of her sisters to marry and have a child. Anyway, we left Dad in Germany for his final two months of service. He hadn't joined the Church at this point, although he did attend each Sunday and loved to associate with the members and the full-time missionaries who were stationed there. While we were still there, Mom always had the missionaries over for dinner, sensing how far a little home cooking went and hoping that their influence would rub off on Dad—so they were regular guests in our home.

After we left Germany, unbeknownst to Mom and her family, Dad did something totally unexpected. He invited the missionaries to again give him the discussions so he could determine once and for all if the Church was true and if he should join. He loved stimulating intellectual discussions, and the Bible seemed to provide the best forum for this to take place.

Elders Flannigan and Packer were the missionaries, and they would have to meet with Dad late at night in his office in Zweibruecken. His schedule didn't permit meeting at more normal times, but this seemed agreeable to them, and so the discussions ensued. As Dad relates, this was his first serious investigation of the gospel, since all of his free time allowed him to *think* about what they were teaching. Each time he prayed about his feelings, he felt more and more that what the Church taught was truth.

Then a pivotal moment came. Dad went to Berlin to attend a basketball tournament; while there he decided to visit a library and read everything he could about Mormonism. Some of what he read was published by the Church, and he felt peaceful when reading it. But when he began to read the anti-Mormon literature, his spirit became distressed and angry. He could see the absurdity of the logic used to put down the Church, and in the end it just made him more convinced than ever that the gospel of Jesus Christ had literally been restored to the earth. He began to seriously contemplate his future with his wife and son and the prospect of having them for this life only. The eternities seemed to become much more focused in Dad's sights when he considered the blessing of being sealed to his family forever in an LDS temple. It was an overwhelming confirmation to his prayers, and he knew at that time that he couldn't stay out of the waters of baptism.

Later that night, he called his Mormon friend Jerry Ingalsbee back at his home in Zweibruecken, and told him to get the font ready for his baptism. He knew he was ready and that there was no turning back.

A special baptismal service was held just for him, with his friend Captain Jerry Ingalsbee performing the actual baptism. Elder Packer then confirmed him a member of the Church and bestowed on him the gift of the Holy Ghost.

Following the services, Dad made a phone call to Mom in Castle Dale. When he told her that he had been baptized, she was totally blown away. Her response was quick, however, as she said, "Reiner, you have not! You don't have to call long distance just to tease me about being baptized!" Dad was cool, though, and after some time of insisting that he was telling her the truth, Mom believed him and found herself weeping for joy.

At Last We're Reunited

Not long after this, Dad was discharged from the army and returned home to Castle Dale. Everyone welcomed him with open arms and congratulated him on becoming a Latter-day Saint. He was pretty humbled by all the attention, but with me slobbering on his shirt and with Mom at his side, he pretty much thought he had the world by the tail.

At that time, we moved back to his home, in Reno, Nevada. He still planned to become a doctor and felt this was the place to live while he was being considered for medical school. The best thing that happened to our family while living in Reno was the birth of my younger sister, Tasha. She came into the world 17 July 1974, and I was instantly a very jealous but dedicated older brother.

After eight months in Reno, and after realizing that this profession wasn't opening up to him, Dad and Mom decided to move to Provo, Utah, where he began a second bachelor of science degree, this time in microbiology, focussing on medical technology. His first bachelor's degree from the University of Utah had been in biology, and so this seemed to be a complementary degree to follow up with.

We finally moved, and had our trailer house moved there as well. While Dad was attending school, I was creating my first memories of playing at the Liahona Preschool on about 500 East Center Street. Mom and Dad thought I needed some socializing, since I was so big for my age. I was comfortable playing around kids my own size, but they were all a year or two older than me, and this concerned them enough to get me some added social training.

Becoming Mobile

While living here I also acquired a best friend. We would ride our Big Wheels together, racing up and down the street. It was a blast! When we'd get tired of doing this, we'd play in the sandbox together. Though we spent a lot of time together, Mother's watchful eye always seemed to know what mischief we were getting into. Years later, when I was in high school, Mom informed me that this friend had died of a severe illness, and I just felt terrible. The news of his death was really hard on me.

On my fourth birthday, Mom and Dad thought I was big enough to learn to ride a bike. None of my four-year-old friends had them because they were so little, but my older friends did, and my folks must have thought I could handle one. So, one day right out of the blue, a new 22" one-speed Schwinn bicycle was handed to me. They sat me on it and pushed me, and off I went down the street. I had balance and stayed up without a hitch—well, except that they hadn't told me how to stop. So in a couple of minutes I panicked and crashed onto someone's lawn. They came running, helped me up, and told me how to start and stop. Before long I figured it out, and by the end of the day there wasn't much I couldn't do on that bike. It had to have been one of the happiest days of my life!

Another memory of living in Provo involved the times Dad and I would take a walk down to the train tracks. There was a bridge there, and we'd walk across the bridge, always looking over our shoulders to make sure a train wasn't coming. It probably wasn't that big a bridge, but in my three- and four-year-old mind, it was pretty scary. Our best times there would be in placing coins on the tracks so they'd get smashed out flat with the passing of the next train. We did this a lot, and although the coins would usually fall off as soon as the first wheels hit them, two or three times they stayed, and after the train passed we'd peel the smashed coin off the track and take it home. Were we ever heroes then!

Perhaps I should mention here that at between the ages of two and four, I learned how to drive—and how to wear out trucks. I drove so hard that I actually wore out three trucks during those years. They were the giant yellow Tonka trucks, actually, and could I ever make them hum! I'd get a hand on each side, lean over, and then bear down while running down a sidewalk at full speed. Now, that was fun! I actually wore the tires off again and again. The rims would also break, and when that happened, we'd take it to Grandpa Wilberg, who'd get out his welding torch and weld them back on. I think this is where I learned to play with intensity. I knew no middle speed, and the word *slow* wasn't even in my dictionary.

In 1976, as Dad completed his degree and was just finishing his internship as a medical technologist, we went on a family trip back to Castle Dale. He met with the officials at the Emery County Medical Center, and they told him that they had just recently been considering hiring a medical technologist. Dad turned to Mom and smiled, and then the administrator said, "Well, Reiner, it looks like you're hired." Anticipation of a secure job offer must have been a big relief for both Mom and Dad.

On 11 November of that year, just a month before our return to Castle Dale, my little brother, Justin, was born. I'll never forget going with Dad and Tasha up to the Utah Valley Hospital in Provo and seeing Justin for the first time. He was a handsome little guy, but he had a hard time opening his eyes. I was proud to at last have a little brother to play with.

Now that Justin was born, Mom and Dad were thrilled that they could return to Mom's roots with such a great professional opportunity offered them. And so, after Dad completed his internship in Provo, they packed up their belongings and three kids (actually we were just part of their belongings), and moved to Castle Dale.

That first year in the valley, we lived in Grandpa Wilberg's old white house, three miles north of town on his ranch. Actually, we moved the trailer house down and lived in it for a month first. But then Dad sold it, and we moved into what is called the ranch house.

While living there, I mostly played and got the hang of ranching at my Grandpa's side. Mom and Dad, on the other hand, built their own home across the street and down the road a piece. Grandpa had given them ten acres on which to settle, and they did it with gusto. Although I was too young to appreciate how skilled Dad was, after the house had been framed, he and Mom went to work and completely built the rest of it. He custom built the kitchen and bathroom cabinets, wired the house, put in the plumbing, put on the shingles, and hung the sheetrock. He rightfully boasted that if he could read a set of plans, he could build anything.

Finally, after a full year of Mom and Dad working well into the night (after he had worked all day at the medical center), our family moved into our new home. The total square footage was 1,200 square feet on the main floor, with an unfinished basement. We were the most fortunate family around, but we didn't have any close neighbors—except for cattle, pheasants, and prairie dogs.

We were excited to be in our new home, and soon a small shed and corral were finished behind the house. That meant our cow could become a permanent resident. I'm not sure when I began milking, but it was too early, I'm sure of that! Other chores were always waiting as well, and I grew up learning the value of hard work.

Such were the early days of my youth, as I gained in wisdom and stature—actually in strength and stature. And in such a frame of mind, I began to anticipate life in the fast lane. Kindergarten was just around the corner—or about three miles down the road—and I couldn't wait to begin!

3

Teams, Talents, and Tendonitis

Entering Kindergarten

Beginning elementary school was big potatoes for me, and I could hardly wait for the first day to arrive. Mom bought me new school clothes, and I even got a haircut to commemorate the occasion. Although the bus was scheduled to pick me up at the end of our lane and take me to the school, on the first day Mom took me just to make sure I found my new classroom okay.

In the neighboring town of Ferron, another kindergarten boy also started school that day. His name was Jason Nelson, and he was also tall for his age. In the years to come, he would become one of my best friends, but at this time we had not yet met. Although I didn't know it at the time, his mother assisted with the registration at our school. When registration was completed, she returned home surprised and told her husband, who would later become my high school basketball coach, that Jason was only the second-tallest person in the county to enroll in kindergarten.

A couple of weeks later, Jason's dad, whom I later came to know as J.R., measured us, and Jason actually came up to my chin. Jason would eventually reach the height of 6'7", but this "moment of measuring" was the beginning of my notoriety as a tall person. It was also when Mom and Dad reinforced how proud I should be that I was tall, even though some unkind things had been spoken about my height. I took their words to heart, and from that time forth was proud to stand up straight, square my shoulders, and be proud of what the Lord had given me.

While I don't remember a great deal about my first year in school, I do recall loving to have our teacher read stories to us. I also loved my blanket and the rest we took each day after eating our milk and cookies.

When it came time to rest, I'd lie on my blanket and close my eyes, faking sleep. Our teacher would give us a star for our forehead when we went to sleep, and of course I wanted to obey. But my mind was so full of exciting things to do—both with my new friends and back on the farm—that I just couldn't relax enough to sleep. So I lay quietly, pretending to be in never-never land, never imagining that the teacher really knew. One time I pulled it off, too, because when we "woke up," sure enough I was awarded a star. At the time, I thought how cool I was wearing that bright red star. Looking back on it, I think nap time was more for the teacher than for the kids. We were a pretty rowdy bunch, and I think she just needed a few minutes to relax so she could cope with the rest of the day!

My other memory of kindergarten was reading time in the kiva, or pit. We had a circle that was lower than the other area, like an Anasazi Indian kiva. We'd sit down there while the teacher would read us a story, and it was awesome. Those are favorite memories.

Attending the Castle Dale Elementary School became my life's focus. Mr. Jorgensen was our principal, and even though he seemed like an old man, he was good to me, so that made everything all right. Ann Jorgensen, his sister-in-law, was my kindergarten teacher, and at the end of the year my progress report listed all S's. It was the highest grade I could get, and on the report she wrote these words: "Promoted to first grade. Great improvement! Shawn has really matured! He still hits and hurts others frequently, but is generally improving."

When I took my report card home, I felt bad that I was thought of as a bully, and after Mom and Dad gave me a good dose of parental love, I vowed to be *kinder and gentler*. I think my resolve may have worked, too, because the next year, under

Catherine Nelson's teaching, I received only *excellents* and *satisfactorys*, with not one *needs improvement*. I wasn't perfect by any means, but my social skills were definitely on the upswing.

Mrs. Jorgensen's nephew Josh became my very best friend in grade school, and he and I were totally cool together. We had great times. Josh's cousin Joseph, Shane Miller, and Ryan Peacock were also good friends. We were also in the same CTR (Choose the Right) class at church, so we were definitely "tight." Tyler Wilstead was also a good friend, but he was in another ward.

On a lighter side, when I was eight or nine, Josh and I somehow "procured" a string of firecrackers. We got on our bikes and rode down Main Street in Castle Dale. There's a beer hall there, and we stopped right outside, lit the string of firecrackers, and threw them inside through the front door that was always open for circulation. We were actually riding past when we threw them, and we took off, rounded the corner, and hightailed it down the street so we wouldn't get caught. We didn't get caught, either, and we've often laughed about how daring we were, and how surprised those folks were. They must have thought World War III was starting! Now, that was fun, even though looking back on it, it surely was a reckless thing to do.

It seems ironic, but on the other side of the coin, I'll always remember working for an entire week doing jobs around the house so I could earn twenty-five cents with which to buy my CTR ring. This was a small ring that our Church Primary, or children's organization, offers and is worn as a reminder to make correct choices. That was the most important thing in the world to me, and was I ever proud when I received it and put it on my finger. I think it helped me want to choose the right, too, even though I'd have momentary lapses with firecrackers, because on most days I tried awfully hard to live up to what it meant.

I got involved in another activity that reinforced the Choose the Right program, and that was with Zachery and Adam Rogers, friends from California, who had come to visit us. One day, quite innocently, we armed ourselves with huge, fully loaded squirt guns. Then we went to the Wilberg Wash Bridge across from our home and hunkered down out of site, waiting for a car to come by. One did, all right, and we rose up with perfect timing and let the water fly. Our aim was sure, and with perfect trajectory the water landed all over the windshield of the passing car. We had only one problem—riding in the car was our local policeman. He slammed on his brakes, backed up, and before we knew it was standing over us, more upset than a cow past milking time. When I saw his light flashing, I knew we were in "deep wash" trouble. That officer gave us the Scotch blessings of our lives for doing such a dangerous thing, and I vowed then and there that I had just squirted my last windshield.

Now let me share how good I was. The highlight of my second grade was in being chosen to take a part in our class play, *Hansel and Gretel*. Because of my height, or my acting skills, I'm not sure which, I was asked to play the part of a tree. For me, that was a great honor, and I took my part very seriously.

Our Family Cabin in Joe's Valley

Ever since I can remember, even when we were still living in Provo, we've made our family retreat up in Joe's Valley. During those early years, Dad and his brother Pete, Mom's sisters and their husbands, and Grandpa and Grandma would spend a week at a time up there, building what would become our summer cabin. They formed the foundation for the cabin from four wooden power poles that had broken off at the base and blown down in a recent windstorm. Grandpa bought these broken poles from the power company, and they were perfect for the job. They were huge, and Dad was forced to use a logging pick and tractor to move them into place at the cabin site. He and the others then used poles from an old abandoned telephone line that ran through Grandpa's property to build the walls of the cabin.

Once it was built, this cabin became a frequent retreat for our family, and as the years have passed, we've stashed more memories at that place than we could ever recount.

Adrianne's Birth

About two and a half months after my eighth birthday, I became a big brother for the third and final time. Mom had been expecting another baby, and Tasha, Justin, and I couldn't wait to see who the Lord was going to send to us. Finally, after it seemed like we had waited forever, Mom announced it was time for her delivery. Dad packed her things, and they lit out for the hospital in Provo. Her doctor practiced there and had delivered Justin, so it was worth the hour-and-a-half drive to have him deliver her next baby. They were fortunate to arrive in time, and before long Dad called and announced to us that we had a new baby sister named Adrianne. The date was 9 June 1980, and were we ever happy! Little did I realize, as an eight-year-old, how much Adrianne would come to mean to me in the years to follow.

Growing Older

Following the summer between third and fourth grade, the local newspaper interviewed several of us about our feelings about going back to school. Never one to hold back, I was quoted as saying, "I feel pretty good about going back. I like math and just about everything." They also interviewed my little sister Tasha, who was going into the second grade. When asked why she wanted school to start, she smiled and said, "I like to color and play."

The reporter took a picture of both of us at the swimming pool, with a towel draped around us, and I guess they caught us in a good mood for us to have made those comments. Actually, I did like school. I was beginning to get some unspoken respect from my peers—both because of my size and my athletic abilities—and at that point I was convinced I could do anything.

Doing the Chores

Ever since I can remember, feeding the animals in the corral behind our house has been a twice-a-day activity. Central to these memories are those of milking our cow, whom Aunt Sandra and Uncle Merrill had affectionately named Olive. Twice a day I'd grab the bucket and do the milking. First I'd pour her a bucket of oats, after which I'd turn the feeding bucket upside down and use it to sit on while doing the milking. This job began every morning at six o'clock, which during the winter months was pretty hard. I'd get bundled up against the cold— which once dipped to twenty-seven degrees below zero—go out and do the milking, then come back in and strain the milk. After that I'd wash up, eat breakfast, and head on out the door for basketball practice, and then for school. Then that night, no matter what time I got home, I would repeat the process.

One night, when I was late going out to milk, Olive was hollering, and Mom said, "Shawn, you get on out there and milk her. You have no idea how badly she's hurting." Mom then explained how it was with her, when she was nursing one of us kids and we didn't want to eat. That put a whole new perspective on milking for me, and I was a lot more punctual after that.

Dad would help me out when I was involved in a game or something, but it seemed like I was always out there milking that cow. In fact, I hated it so bad that I vowed to have a cow for my own boys to milk, just so they could learn to hate it as much as I did. Actually, I learned a lot of lessons with that twice-a-day job, and I'd be less than a good father by not providing my sons with the same "opportunity."

Another chore I hated was weeding our garden. It seems like I never could go any place without Mom or Dad saying, "You can't go until you've gone out and weeded a row in the garden." Sometimes, just to spite them, I'd pull out a couple of plants. I can't believe now that I did that, but at the time it seemed to be the only course of getting even with them for always putting the screws to me.

I did have my moments of recreation, however, especially in the winter. Often this meant simply exploring, even if it didn't involve common sense and obedience. One time, when I was about twelve years old, I invited my friends Scott and Tyler Wilstead to go exploring with me. Now, I had been told a hundred times, if not once, to never walk out on Clay's Pond, because the ice didn't freeze deep enough to withstand body weight. But on this day I figured I knew more than my folks, so I convinced my friends that it would be adventurous for us to test out the ice on the pond. It certainly looked as if it had frozen over at least a foot below the surface.

So, Scott and Tyler bravely followed me out onto the pond, and before we knew it, we were inching closer and closer to the middle. Just at that moment when I knew I had wisdom and perspective far greater than my folks, the ice below our feet began to crack. We froze, looked at each other in horror, and then took off for our lives! The ice cracked with us all the way back to dry ground, and when our feet landed on the frozen shoreline, we were three relieved and repentant explorers. It was years after this near catastrophe that I became brave enough to tell my folks, but when it happened, I taught myself a real good lesson about doing what I had been told.

Being a Cub Scout

I had become a Cub Scout at the age of eight, and had progressed through the ranks of Bobcat, Wolf, and Bear and had become a Webelos Scout. I was really into it. As I mentioned in chapter 2, Dad had become an Eagle Scout while in his youth, and I wanted to do everything I could in Cubs so I would be prepared to enter Scouting. I earned all of the possible arrows and even earned the Arrow of Light award, which is the comparable award to Eagle in the Scouting program. I'll have to give my mom credit for making sure I was where I was supposed to be all the time, and for having a mentality to make sure I did the work and passed off the million requirements. It also helped to have friends who were involved, and we had some great times together.

My Best Friend, Apache

One of the most exciting days of my life was when Grandpa Wilberg gave me my very own pinto horse named Apache. I learned to ride him well, and we became so much a team that he could anticipate when I was going to pull the reins and would turn before I had a chance to do it. We were inseparable, and I'm not exaggerating in saying that he was my totally best friend. I'm not sure he appreciated how heavy I was, and how my legs dangled way down over his sides, but he never complained. Instead, he'd be totally energized whenever I'd climb on for a ride.

It was a sad day when Apache got an infection on his hoof and Dad had to get a vet to examine him. I was hopeful that everything would turn out okay, but we learned that he had cancer, so we had to sell him. This nearly killed me to see my best friend leave, knowing that he would have to be "put to sleep," but I had learned that this was the way of things on the farm, so I gradually adjusted to not having him around. Looking back, I'll have to say that Apache was responsible for more hours of sheer joy in my youth than anything else. He was just the best, and I hope there's a spirit world for animals so I can one day greet him again.

Waxing Creative

Before entering fifth grade, and I guess in an effort to help me improve my handwriting skills, which I *still* haven't mastered, I wrote a special letter to my folks. It was dated 25 July 1982 and read:

> Dear Mom and Dad,
>   I admire you very much for all you do for me. I love you very much. I'll try to obey you as long as I can.
>
>   Your son
>   Shawn

I'm not sure whether I was looking for extra cookies that day or whether I had a plan of disobedience that I had to strategize, but I do know it was a real letter, and I have been thankful that Mom kept it for me.

Sixth grade was a banner year for me. In addition to participating in the county basketball league, I began to experience feelings about things around me. I was also given the assignment of writing a book about different topics, and because this was my first real creative effort, I thought I would share a selection of these topics at this time:

The Boy and the Dog

Once upon a time there was a boy that was sitting on a stool next to a dog. He was in the orchard. He had some medicine in one hand and a teaspoon in the other. I think he was going to give the dog the medicine. He might have had to take some himself. His dog was bundled up and it looked sick. He didn't look too happy to give his dog the medicine. "Oh well."

By Shawn Bradley

On Halloween Night

On Halloween night I was carrying my jackolantern up to the attic window. As I reached the top of the stairs, I dropped my flashlight and it went out! I turned to put the pumpkin down on a table when something grabbed my leg! I screamed as loud as I could but nobody heard me. I looked down and saw a very big brown hairy hand. And then I saw another hand, then a head and even its whole body. It was 6 1/2 feet tall whatever it was. I started to run but it stopped me. I didn't know what to do. It told me to be quiet so I did. It told me its story. Its name was Fred in English. He was from another planet and was a nice beast. It told me about its life and how its people betrayed him and made him come to earth. He told me that he had about 14 friends and they all loved him. He asked me if I could help to get him back home. I said I'll do the best I can. So I worked for about six months. But it didn't work. So I tried again and again. Finally I made something that would work. And it did. I felt very sad that he was leaving. But he told me that he had a machine that would let me go there any time and let him come here any time. So it wasn't so bad after all. Now I see him every week and we have the funnest time together.
The End

By Shawn Bradley

I won't share any more of my stories at this time (but if you are interested, I may just publish them in the near future). All I know is that I enjoyed writing—both prose and poetry. In fact, I have to share just one of my poems with you. It was a Halloween poem, was accompanied by pictures of ghosts and bats and things, and went like this:

Halloween Poem

Halloween people are great in a crate.
They just sit and spit
Until they croak and sometimes even choke.
Halloween people are great in a crate.

In addition to writing, by this time I was also learning to enjoy reading. In fact, one of my prized possessions is a large silver ribbon and medallion that I received for participating in the March of Dimes Reading Olympics. When I received it, I couldn't have been more proud. In my earlier years, I played basketball outside rather than read, and although I don't regret playing ball, I always felt like I was playing catch-up with a book. But, for those of you who are young and are reading *this* book, I can see that this misplaced priority isn't a problem. Just keep setting reading goals, and you'll get more mileage out of it as you grow older than you can ever imagine at this time of your life.

In addition to reading and writing, I also enjoyed acting. Besides taking the part of the tree in my first play, I moved on and increased in talent with later plays. By the time I was in the sixth grade, I had earned the right to play the preacher in *Tom Sawyer.*

This year also opened another horizon to me as I joined our school band. I played the drums and cymbals, and when we had our spring concert in March, I thought I was in rare form. My family attended to support me, and after we had played our numbers I felt like I had really accomplished something.

By the time I completed sixth grade, under the tutelage of Ms. Barbara Curtis, I had no problem taking my report card home. I received mostly A's and B's that year, with straight A's in spelling. My most difficult area was handwriting, where I received C's and B's. I couldn't figure out why this was so important, though, since you didn't need to write in order to milk a cow, brand a calf, or bounce a ball.

I almost forgot to mention that the previous three years had seen another interest take root within my heart. Girls! While many of them were my friends, having our class dances sort of put them on my frontal lobe. Why, you ask? Because I was required to fill out a dance card before each dance, and then to dance with each of the girls on my card. There was no way out of it, and even though I felt like I was all legs and feet, I stumbled through it and did my duty. I probably ruined all the girls' shoes by stepping on them with my huge feet, but they were good sports about it and didn't say much. Come to think of it, they didn't say much of anything. They just sort of looked at my shirt, or at the other kids, and we danced along in agonizing silence.

Those first dances were sheer torture, believe me, but as time went on I actually began to enjoy myself. For example, in the fourth grade Valentine's Day dance, I signed up and danced with nine girls. A year later, I added some extra lines to my card, and danced with fifteen girls. Then in the sixth grade, we had two dances, and again I maxed out my card.

Receiving the Aaronic Priesthood

The highlight of my life to this point took place following my twelfth birthday. At that time, I was interviewed by my bishop, LaVon Day, and was found worthy to receive the Aaronic Priesthood and to be ordained to the office of a deacon. After our ward members gave me a sustaining vote, my family joined with the bishopric in the actual ordination. Those attending who held the priesthood gathered around me in a circle and placed their hands on my head, just as the Apostles of old did when conferring the priesthood. Dad then served as voice, and with the priesthood he held, he conferred the Aaronic Priesthood upon my head and then gave me a blessing that would help me throughout my life.

While I don't recall the particulars of that blessing, I do remember him blessing me with the desire to serve a mission for the Lord and to marry in the temple when the right time arrived. The other thing I remembered is how great I felt as I hugged everyone afterward, knowing that I was now worthy and had the authority to pass the sacrament of the Lord's Supper. As is true for most Latter-day Saint young men, this is a moment and a feeling that I'll never forget.

My other memory of that event was receiving a package in the mail from my grandmother Oma, who was not a member of our Church but was totally supportive of our beliefs. The package contained a tie clasp of the Salt Lake LDS temple, and I wore it with great pride.

Further School Activities

Not long after I received the priesthood, our school held our annual awards assembly. At this time I received a certificate of merit for my athletic skills, and a fourth-place certificate for the all-school chess championship. I was pretty proud of those certificates, and of course Mom took them home and immediately put them in my scrapbook. Actually, she put them next to my certificates of the previous years—namely, third place in checkers, third grade; second place in checkers, fourth grade; and finally third place in checkers, fifth grade. I mastered checkers, I tell you, and even gained a proficiency in chess.

The best part of my report card that year read as follows: "Shawn has been really well behaved. He is a mature student, and is doing well. . . . Have a great summer! Miss ya!" All I could think of was, "Look out, junior high, here I come!"

Summer Fun

To celebrate the coming of the Mormon pioneers to Utah in 1847, our area has hosted an annual July 24th celebration. This year was no exception, and I entered the pie eating contest, thinking it would be a great way to fill up on something tasty. I filled up, all right, but I also did it in record time, taking first place. My award was a giant Pac Man ribbon, designating me as the "No. 1 Pie Eater."

While these times were great, they don't represent the

main focus of my time. That was with Grandpa, ranching. It seems like he'd come by every morning and announce that it was time to do this or that. Often it was to drive up to Joe's Valley and turn the water. I'd light up when we'd go up there, because usually on our way back to the ranch he'd announce that we were stopping for a treat at a small mountain cafe called the Sportsman's Lodge. I remember holding my breath until he said we were going to stop. I also remember working extra hard, just so he'd think I had done enough to warrant a drink or something at the lodge. When he didn't have time to stop, it would almost kill me. Those rides down off the mountain were especially painful if we hadn't gotten a treat.

But it sure was great, being with Grandpa Wilberg. Because his only children were his four daughters, he was happy to have a grandson—the first boy in his posterity. He had even flown all the way to Germany when I was born, just to see me. He brought me a pair of cowboy boots when he came, which started me from day one with a cowboy's mentality.

One of the moments of trust between Grandpa and me was when he would let me carry his pocketknife. He knew how much I loved that knife, even though I always seemed to be losing it. He'd have patience with me, and before long we'd find it—usually sticking in a bail of hay. I felt totally grown up having it in my pocket and used it regularly to cut twine.

When Mom and her sisters were growing up, they were the ranch hands. They helped drive tractor for the hay harvesters, fed the cattle their grain and hay, and helped Grandpa whenever it was time to irrigate or take the water turn. Now their jobs turned to me, and I just grew up knowing what had to be done. When I was too little to drive the tractor, I'd climb up and sit next to Grandpa as we'd bale hay, cut it, and then haul it to the haystack. I don't really remember how old I was when I started driving the tractor alone, but I do know I was young. But I was big enough to handle it, so some of my early memories are of driving that tractor around the ranch.

I never did get in any accidents on that tractor, although I must have come awfully close at times. But I did get in accidents with the animals. I was bucked off my horse a few times, and run over by cattle. One time a bull butted me right in the back, and the pain nearly killed me. I wanted to shoot that bull right there and then, but since I didn't have a rifle, I let him go, vowing that if he ever got mean with me again, it would be the last time.

One of the big hazards of working on a ranch is dealing with barbed wire. It was no exception for me, and it seems like I was always getting cut on that wire. Needless to say, I soon learned to be careful when I was anywhere near that fence.

One of the big problems of running a cattle ranch was in calving. When a baby calf was born and the mother died, or if the mother had twins, we'd have to find a substitute mother for one of the calves to take its milk from. Usually we'd attach it to our milk cow, but sometimes we'd have to bottle-feed it. Mixing up that milk was one of my least favorite jobs, because that powdered stuff was a real mess, and if I didn't clean it all up, I'd surely hear about it from Mom.

In addition to ranch work, sports, and celebrations, I also entered our dog, Sheba, in the county fair dog show. She was a Great Dane (brindle) dog, and won two second places and one first-place ribbon. It was a sad day, several months later, when Sheba died. She had been a true friend to me, and I knew I would really miss her.

My First Try at Sports

Let me go back now to the beginning of organized athletics for me. I don't want to bore anyone with details, so I'll just give a broad brush stroke and share the highlights.

My first memory of sports was actually in Provo, when I was still three years old. Dad would take me to the Joseph Fielding Smith Field House, where he'd run on the track. I'd run with him, and then when we were finished, he'd strap me into my seat that he had rigged on his ten-speed bike and away we'd go. At the time I didn't know we were at the Smith Field House, but when I later went there as a Cougar, the light went on, and I remembered that this was where we had run the track some fifteen years earlier.

As far as basketball is concerned, my very first Christmas present was a new basketball. Dad wanted me to get the hang of it, visually, and I used to palm the ball when the ball would sit on the floor next to me. Then I'd scoot it across the floor, having the time of my life. When Tasha finally got old enough, we'd sit on the floor and scoot it to each other—and that was when she really became an asset in my life.

As first grade came to an end, Mom and Dad signed me up to play T-ball, and was I ever excited! I belted that ball hard, and because I was so much bigger than everyone else, it usually sailed way out into the outfield. I was assigned to play shortstop, since I was the only player who could throw the ball clear over to first base. We were the Castle Dale Cougars, and when the season ended, we had a perfect 9-0 record. More important than our record was the fact that I had begun to think of myself as a champion. It wasn't so much of a "being superior" kind of mind-set but rather a feeling that there wasn't anything I couldn't achieve if I set my heart to it.

Playing baseball pretty much became my spring activity from then on, and our little league seasons just got better and better. Bill Dye, who was in our ward, was my baseball coach for as many years as I could remember. He was fantastic and taught me almost everything I knew about the game. We did have one problem, however, and that was when Coach Dye bought a new shell for his pickup. He had it over to the side of the field, and we were up batting. He was standing by his truck with the back window up, visiting with my dad, and when a boy fouled the ball quite close to the truck, he told my dad that he ought to put the window down so it wouldn't get hit. As luck would have it, I was the next batter up, and wouldn't you know it if I didn't hit a foul ball that went up, up, up . . . and then finally came down right on top of that plastic window. It just shattered it to pieces. Coach Dye looked at me, and I looked at him, and I thought I was dead. He controlled himself, though, and because it was an accident, he paid for a new one to be installed.

I pitched quite a bit, mostly sidearm, and I think I did a pretty good job at the mound. I also moved from shortstop to first base when I wasn't pitching, and that was great also. Batting was the part of the game, though, that I think I enjoyed most of all. I remember one day, when I was about ten years old and our team was playing a game over in Orangeville, just a mile or so west of Castle Dale. I was batting, and a lady yelled out from the stands that she'd buy me a soda pop every time I hit a home run. She was one of the mothers, I guess, and wanted to motivate me so her son could win. Anyway, every time I got to bat, I hit a home run—three for the game. Each time, off she'd go to buy me another can of pop.

Finally, after buying the third drink, she asked me to slack off a bit so she wouldn't have to buy any more. Well, by then the game was about over, so I didn't get back to bat. I'll say this, when we drove home afterward, my stomach was sloshing around like a washing machine. But was I ever happy, enjoying the rewards of a game well played!

Summer Basketball Camps

One of my favorite memories through grade school was the annual summer basketball camp conducted by Jason Nelson's dad, known affectionately as "J.R." Coach Nelson always encouraged me to play with kids older than me. He told my folks that he did this for two reasons: one, so that I could play with kids of my own skill level, and two, so that the other kids my age wouldn't feel badly about me dominating the game.

One day, when I had been working on a special project at the ranch, I was late for practice. Coach Nelson really stressed punctuality, and I always tried to get to practice or a game on time. But on this day I couldn't, and when I arrived and was tying my shoelaces, he came up to me and spoke quite firmly, "Shawn, where have you been?"

I had been told to always tell the truth, and so I said, "I've been helping my grandpa put in some culverts, and we didn't get done in time."

Coach Nelson knew of my relationship with my grandpa, so instead of scolding me for being late, he smiled and said, "Well, I'm sure he couldn't have done it without you."

I was relieved that I hadn't been fussed at or that he hadn't made me run a couple of laps for being late, but even more than that I was happy that I had been truthful and that he had believed me. His response made me want to always tell the truth and has stuck with me to this day.

During fourth grade, I had another new experience with our 4-H club. They held a one-on-one basketball competition, and I won at the region level. This qualified me for the state competition at Utah State in Logan, so our family drove up there so I could compete. I knew I would win the first-place trophy, so to humble me, a tiny little guy beat me by two points in the finals. I couldn't handle the defeat, and I just cried and cried. My folks did some serious talking to me about losing gracefully, I remember that.

As time passed, I continued to grow at a phenomenal rate, and my skills improved right along with it. I really didn't perceive myself as going through an awkward stage, although I must have looked like a giant daddy longlegs spider at times. I was teased at times about being so tall and skinny, but I didn't mind. My folks had always taught me to stand up straight and be proud of my height, and that mentality sort of stuck with me.

Fifth Grade, Reaching Six Feet in Height

As the new year began, in 1983, I had the opportunity of a lifetime. My Uncle Duane took me to Salt Lake City, and we watched the Utah Jazz play the Boston Celtics. I truly thought I had died and gone to heaven, sitting there in the Salt Palace watching players of that caliber battle it out on the hardwood. I knew life didn't get any better than that! In fact, I enjoyed it so much that Coach Bob Starr, from our all-star team, gave me two discarded play-off tickets for my scrapbook. This was the first year that the Jazz made the play-offs, and was I ever psyched!

This was also the time for me to again join the county little league basketball program. Dad was our team coach, and we had a super team. Our final record was six wins against three loses, and I had a season high of 26 points. In one game, we won 26-19, and I scored 24 of our points. I don't think the other players hardly ever shot the ball, though, as they just threw it in to me for the easy lay-up. I was so much taller than anyone else that it wasn't really fair. I didn't know that then, however, as I just thought it was an opportunity I could take advantage of.

Toward the end of the fifth grade, I was again invited to participate in the 4-H one-on-one basketball competition. I took first place again in the Green River region, and then our family traveled again to Utah State University for the state competition. This year I placed first, winning three out of three games. For the championship, I beat a different boy than the one who had beaten me the year before, and it felt great. That guy had been beaten out in the semifinals. I measured at just under six feet tall, and I was excited to win a basketball auto-graphed by the USU Aggie team, a T-shirt, and a 4-H hat. I was also happy for Travis Wakefield, from Huntington, who also competed and who made it into the semifinals. Our families had a great time, and it felt super bringing the state championship back to Castle Dale. There were no tears after that competition, I assure you.

Following fifth grade, I was assigned to the Dodgers little league baseball team, and we had a great year, taking the league championship. I also had a good year, personally. My season batting average was .433. Hitting the ball was becoming easier and easier, and because my size was somewhat intimidating at the plate, the pitcher usually threw at least one ball I could hit. That summer I was selected to play for the city all-stars, and we had the time of our lives.

As fall approached, I was excited to sign up for the county rec football program, and when they handed out the uniforms, I was given the number 74. I became a member of the Colt's team and played quarterback. This was the first time I had put on pads. My greatest fun was in faking a handoff, then throwing the ball to a receiver. Because I was so much taller than anyone else, the ball would sail over their outstretched hands, and either be caught or dropped—or overthrown, of course. I even ran the ball now and then, and when I was tackled, I always stretched out, knowing that would give our team a few extra yards. Another one of those benefits of being so "stretched out."

Following football season, we took a short break and then went right into basketball. By this time I was really on fire about playing basketball, and I lived and breathed it every day of my life. Grandpa Wilberg had built an old wooden back-board and had crafted a metal hoop that he attached to it. Then he installed it on an old telephone pole, and it became a great basketball standard for my Mom and her sisters to play on when they were growing up. One day I asked him if we could move it over to our property so I could get more practice time in. He would do just about anything for me, and before I knew it, I had my very own hoop! Grandpa was always the greatest for helping us get what we needed.

As time passed, I grew, and the basket rim got closer and closer to me. I played ball every day, even in the dead of winter, and whenever Mom would need me, she'd always know where I would be.

I'd get the cow milked and the rest of the chores finished, then I'd shovel off the snow in front of the hoop and shoot until it was too dark to see the basket. Mom was always worried that I'd catch pneumonia out in that cold, but I didn't care. I knew what made me happy, and that was playing imaginary games against worthy opponents, twelve months of the year! In the summertime, I would rake the dirt to keep the rocks off the court before every game. Several years later, when Mom and Dad had some extra money, they poured me a *real* court out of concrete and installed a new basketball standard. When I began to touch the rim and dunk the ball, I was always breaking the rim. Grandpa didn't mind, though, and it seemed like either he or Dad was always welding it back together so I could continue to practice. This court is where we still play today, and it'll always be there for me whenever I'm home in Castle Dale.

Organized Basketball

I started playing basketball in the county rec league when I turned eight. Dad coached our team for the first two years, and I thought I was pretty special having him as our coach. That first year we'd mostly run up and down the court, dribble until the ball was taken away, and once in a while get a shot in. The guards did get the ball in to me on occasion, and I usually went in for an uncontested lay-up. Once in a while I even got to shoot from outside, and so I felt good about how my game was progressing. My Mom was always in the stands supporting me, too, and her yelling and clapping was great encouragement.

My first basketball coaches included Kent Keele, Bill Dye, Bill Jorgensen, and my dad. Each in his own way taught me a great deal, and I'll always be thankful for what I learned from them. In those days, it seems that we were always dribbling around chairs and doing drills that had nothing to do with the hoop. Now, in looking back, I can see how these drills gave me the confidence I would later need to dribble the ball. I won't detail our teams and these years. I'll leave it with the fact that we usually won the league championship, and I have more trophies than I'll ever know what to do with.

Developing a Point Guard Mentality

Participating in all-star camps both during the school year and in the summer was becoming more and more meaningful to me. One of the best camps was held locally, with Coach Bob Starr in a traveling Utah Jazz youth development camp. Coach Starr was a recent convert to the LDS faith, having joined the Church the previous January in Gotenborg, Sweden. As a result of joining the Church, he left a very prestigious international coaching career in Europe and South America to come to Utah and see how the Mormon culture fit. He was acclaimed throughout the world as one of the most knowledgeable coaches in the history of the game. An Argentine newspaper was quoted, saying that Coach Starr was "the greatest coach" the country had ever had. The *Daily Herald,* in Provo, quoted him as saying, "I'd like to stay in basketball and show young people it can change their lives. I won, and I never knew I could win at anything. I'd like to work with underprivileged youth. I know I can help somebody win."

Coach Starr brought this winning attitude to Emery County, and his camps became pretty important to my development—both as a person and as a player. The first time I went to Starr's camp I had one of the most significant events of my entire basketball career. It's why I think of myself as a tall point guard rather than as a center who can't handle the ball. Coach Starr informed me that he wasn't going to allow me to play the center position—that is, not until I reached the height of 6'8". I was surprised when he told me this, but then he told me that I had a natural ability with the ball and that if I was going to become a complete player, I had to learn the point guard position. He told me that whenever I came to his camp, this would be where I played, until I reached that magical height.

So, trusting in his philosophy, I worked with the other

guards, dribbling between my legs, behind my back, shooting from outside, dishing off without looking at the intended receiver—essentially all of the basic skills that a guard running the offense had to know. I even learned to have a court awareness that guards had to have—knowing where each of the other four players were, anticipating their moves, and so forth. Since this early hour, while in junior high school, I have maintained this mentality, and I know I'm a better player because of it. Even so, I'll have to secretly admit that a couple of years later, when I finally went to his camp at a height of 6'8", I was relieved that he let me play center and that I could learn from him the skills of that position.

Track Competition

While we were always having running contests, it was not until the fourth grade that I was officially old enough to participate in the Castle Dale track and field meet. I did this for the next three years, and earned the following ribbons each of those years:

Fourth grade—1st place in 100-yard dash and long jump
    2nd place in high jump
    3rd place in 60-yard dash
    4th place in 440-yard relay
    5th place in 880-yard relay

Fifth grade—1st place in long jump, 880-yard run, 100-yard dash, softball throw, and 440-yard run
    2nd place in high jump and 440-yard relay
    3rd place in 60-yard dash

Sixth grade—1st place in 440-yard run (school record), softball throw, and long jump
    2nd place in 880-yard run
    3rd place in 440-relay
    5th place in 100-yard dash
    6th place in 60-yard dash

Looking back on those track and field days, I can hardly believe how many events I participated in. I can also see a trend of getting better in endurance events, such as the 440-yard run, while watching several of my classmates develop into great sprinters. They probably had to take two steps for every step I took, but they became pretty good at it. Regardless of any advantage my size gave me over my classmates, my competitive nature always drove me to try to win. Still, I never fell short of having a great time.

A Summer of Learning

The week after school let out, I attended Coach J.R. Nelson's Emery Spartan basketball camp at the high school. It was a full week of training and playing, and I gained a great respect for Coach Nelson at that time—both as a coach and as a person. He was just as concerned with our learning about teamwork and unselfishness as he was in teaching us basketball skills. I was about 6'2" by this time, and I found that my added height was becoming more and more of an asset to my playing ability.

Next on my agenda was entering my first tennis tournament, held in conjunction with the county fair. I took second place in that tournament and felt good about my skill development.

San Rafael Junior High School

Being bussed each morning to San Rafael Junior High School in Ferron, some ten miles south of Castle Dale, became my life for the next three years. In addition, I felt like my folks and I were always shuttling back and forth, going to this activity or that. It was fun to be in junior high, and my friends and I were having a blast.

For my junior high years, Coaches Philip Nelson and David Thompson took charge of our teams, and we were all treated like winners. They had great competitive attitudes, regardless of the season and the sport, and as players we worked our hearts out to live up to their expectations.

In addition to school activities and sports, this time for me was also consumed with Scouting. With Dad's encouragement, and with the dedication of my Scout leaders, I attended all of the camporees, Scout camps, and Klondike Derbies I could. I advanced in rank, too, and finally, on 12 November 1985, I received my Eagle Scout award. The certificate was signed by President Ronald Reagan, as honorary president of the BSA, as well as by the other officers.

In all, I had earned twenty-eight merit badges, seven more than the required amount for Eagle. I also felt good about my Eagle service project, where I supervised the planting of three hundred ponderosa pine trees around the Joe's Valley Reservoir campsite area. As I kept track of our service, I was surprised that the other Scouts and I spent a total of eighty-one hours. My scoutmaster, Mike Monfredi, especially worked hard; without him, I don't know if I could have completed it.

More Summer Basketball Camps

After school let out, Mom again enrolled me in J.R. Nelson's basketball camp. He then took us to a team camp, which was held in Price at the College of Eastern Utah. The camp included teams made up of players in all three grades of junior high. Our team didn't have the luxury of practicing before the tournament began, but we still won the tournament championship.

I had an experience with my height at this time that has stayed with me ever since. Some of the losing players in the tournament labeled me "Grasshopper" because I was tall, gangly, and skinny as a rail. Coach J.R. was pretty upset about this, and so he came and spoke to me about my feelings. I told him: "The name calling doesn't bother me, Coach. If those guys don't like my size, that's their problem." It was honestly how I felt, and even though I could understand their frustration in playing against me, I had made up my mind to never make an excuse or be defensive about my height. This was a good moment for me to reinforce that self-concept within myself.

Going into eighth grade was pretty exciting for me, as it all seemed so familiar. Again I was bussed over to Ferron with my Castle Dale classmates, and I knew we were going to have a banner year. I had grown to 6'4" by this time.

This year, in addition to becoming a member of the National Junior Honor Society, I became totally committed to winning the league basketball championship. In a way I even began to expect it, since we had such pure ball players on our team.

My Very First Dunk

It was also during the eighth grade basketball season that I found I could dunk a basketball. At that time, I had just been measured at 6'6", so I was feeling my oats. The dunk actually took place during the halftime warm-ups of a game we were playing, and I just dribbled up to the basket, slammed it down through the net, and then looked around to make sure everyone had seen my feat. What I hadn't planned on, of course, was the referee seeing it. But he did, and I was immediately assessed a technical foul. This ticked me off, since it felt like such an unfair rule. But the coach sat me on the bench to start the quarter, and although we were ahead by 40 points when the quarter began, still I was upset that I had to sit on the bench and think about my technical. Finally, when I was put back in the game, I received quite an ovation for having dunked the ball. I knew I was a hero then and that somehow from that time forth my game would never be the same.

In both the eighth and ninth grades, we took the junior high league championship. In '86, when I was in eighth grade, I played for both the eighth- and ninth-grade teams. On the latter team, we beat the Mont Harmon Pirates 47-37 for the title. The following year, we beat the Canyon View Cougars. They were the host team for the tournament and had beaten us twice during the regular season. Because of their 16-0 record going into the game, they were the number one seed. We were seeded second, but we didn't have a second-place mentality, and we fought our hearts out to win. When the dust settled, we had posted a 68-65 victory, and we were out of our minds with excitement. Ryan Stilson led our team with 21 points, and I had 17. But I especially enjoyed my defensive play, which seemed to give them problems whenever I was in the game. I actually sat out much of the second and third quarters with foul trouble, but the other players picked up the slack, and we weren't to be denied!

Meeting Danny Ainge

One of the friendships that I've appreciated over the past six years is with Danny Ainge, now with the Phoenix Suns. When I was little, I used to watch him play during his years at BYU and then as a starting guard for the Boston Celtics. I loved his affinity for both baseball *and* basketball, and I identified with him because of this. But I also admired his dogged dedication during a game and the attitude he had of winning every game he started. There was just no quit in him. I also admired Danny's character and the fact that he was not afraid for people to know that he was LDS, that he was happily married in the temple, and that he had total moral fiber.

This last fact came to my attention the night I shook his hand and met him for the first time. I was in Provo, attending a professional athletes night in the Marriott Center, when I was in the ninth grade. I was 6'11" at that time, and after Danny and other athletes had spoken, I had the privilege of meeting him personally. He said some awfully kind things to me about my future as a basketball player, and that really impressed me. He didn't want to talk about himself, but just wanted to talk about *me*.

This was a night of learning about professional athletes and what made them succeed in such a heady, corrupt environment, and I'll always appreciate the time Danny took to visit with me.

Ninth-grade Summer Tournaments

At the end of my junior high days, I was happy to begin thinking of high school ball and staying home in Castle Dale to attend Emery High. But for the time being, I was even more excited about the summer basketball camps that I was enrolled in. Coach Nelson was well aware of my previous camps and had done so much for me in his camps, but now he wanted to do more for our team, so he signed us up to participate in the AAU tournaments in Salt Lake City. Perhaps it would be best to share his journal entry, as he records our experience there:

> When Shawn's class became ninth graders, I decided it was time for some real exposure for Shawn. A good

friend and fellow "Ferronite" Mike Killpack of the Salt Lake County Recreation Department kept sending me entries to AAU basketball tournaments in Salt Lake. It was too far to travel every night during the school year, so I never entered a team until Shawn's. It nearly killed us all going to school all day, traveling for three hours, playing a game, getting home at one or two in the morning, then starting all over the next day.

The travel and the sleepless nights finally caught up with us, and we ended up taking second place. Still, Shawn was on TV every night, and then with the AAU All-Stars to the next level of competition. As they say, at that time "A star was born." It was during this competition that I discovered the healthy attitude Shawn's classmates had about his notoriety and fame with the media.

While Shawn was being interviewed on television, I gathered the team under a stairwell for a quick meeting. I told them that this was only the beginning, and that when they got to high school, this notoriety was going to happen all the time. I told them that they had the potential to set high school history by winning championships, but that this was only the beginning for Shawn, and that when they got to high school this was going to happen all the time. I told them that a lot of their future success depended on their attitude about Shawn. If they were happy for him to be getting all the publicity, and weren't jealous of it, they would always be winners.

Steve Gordon, who was destined to win the first of Emery's two state championships with the "miracle shot" from half court, summed up the entire team's feelings when he said, "Isn't it okay to be just a little bit of both?" In other words, weren't feelings of slight envy natural, even while they were supporting Shawn? I assured him that they were, and thanked him and the others for their healthy attitude. This attitude has followed the team, too, and because of it, they have traveled all over the country together, and set records that may never be broken.

On a personal note, as Shawn's advanced placement

Honor's English instructor, I have been amazed at how well he has done. I also observed him as president of the Junior Class, and how he took charge of the activities, especially the Junior Prom. . . . Shawn felt the sense of leadership, and knew that he had a responsibility to oversee [the other officers'] respective assignments. Never once did he allow something to fall through the cracks.

Even today, Shawn continues to amaze me, and I'll always stand a little taller for having known this humble, gentle giant.

As a statement about Coach Nelson, I'll have to say that he taught me as much, if not more, about basketball as anyone. And now, after playing for him in the summer camps throughout my early years, I was really looking forward to being on Emery's varsity team and having him as my head coach. I always felt he brought out the best in my play, but even more than that, he has been concerned for the individual—a true people builder.

That summer I traveled to the Las Vegas AAU tournament as part of the Provo all-star team. Paul Ruffner, former BYU great, was our coach, and we won three games against only one loss. During this trip I developed a friendship with Rob Kimmel, from Provo, that has become more of a brother-to-brother relationship. His folks have also become my parents away from home, and I've always had a pillow to lay my head on in their home.

I also traveled to Phoenix to play in the BCI tournament as part of a New Mexico team. Jerry Chavez was my coach at this tournament, and he really worked to develop me as a player.

Something else happened during the summer that brought me great relief. After wearing braces on my teeth for a full three years, ever since the seventh grade, I was able to get them taken off. During part of this time I had even worn head-gear—with those straps and wires going over the top of my head, around my neck and cheeks, everywhere! It was something awful, a total pain, and I felt like a tagged and branded calf. Luckily, I only had to wear them a short time, and then just around the house.

On a brighter note, as the summer came to a close and I

was able to spend time with my family, ranching, and at our cabin in Joe's Valley, I was totally excited about life. I didn't know what the next three years at Emery High would bring, but I did know how to have fun. Although I was oblivious to the pressures that would be placed on my shoulders with our basketball fortunes, I felt like I was up to the task. It was an awesome thing to consider, but with my friends and teammates at my side, I felt there was nothing we couldn't accomplish.

4

Magical Moments at Emery High

My Sophomore Year

As summer wound down, the thoughts of entering high school began to consume our thinking. My friends and I found ourselves talking more and more about who was going out for the football team. They all were, of course; but my parents and basketball coach, J.R. Nelson, didn't want me to risk injury on the grid iron, so I had to watch from the sidelines. I had grown another two inches and was now 7'1", so I knew I had to be careful.

From this time forth, I resigned myself to be satisfied with participating in the no contact sports, including basketball. I've always been intrigued that basketball is called a no contact sport. From my experience, it's *heavy* contact, and the pros in the NBA have *total* contact! But so much for that.

Our season was great, and when we had finished our final regular season game, we found ourselves with a perfect 18-0 record.

My First Regional Tournament

Going to region was exciting to consider, especially since I had established myself as a starter for varsity. I knew I was playing with some great athletes, but since I had grown up playing with them, and with others older than me, I felt like I fit right in.

Richfield beat us for the regional championship, and I wasn't surprised to learn that Ryan Cuff had made 52 of his team's 64 points, besides having four assists. That meant that Richfield only scored three or four points in the entire game that Ryan wasn't responsible for. He was awesome, playing one of the greatest games I've ever seen. People still say he played possessed and out of his head. As for me, I was just one of the team, with Steven Jorgensen, Jeff Cisneros, Dell and Scott Stilson, and Joel Wilson. These guys were skilled ball players, and I felt fortunate to be playing with them.

The following week we found ourselves in the state 2-A tournament, in Ogden, Utah. Even though we had lost the regional championship to Richfield, we were confident that we would do well. During the state play-offs, we lost one more game. This gave us a third-place finish, with a season record of 22-2.

Grandma Bradley's Death

One of the saddest events of my life was receiving word from Reno, Nevada, that Grandma "Oma" Bradley had died of cancer. She was only sixty-one and months before had seemed totally full of life. Her life had been a difficult one in that she had left her family in Germany to spend a life with Opa in the States. But she had reared a great family, had taught them the teachings of the Savior, and had also become an accomplished librarian. In fact, at the elementary school where she worked, they honored her by naming the Friedl Bradley Library after her. Even though I haven't seen her as often as I did my Wilberg grandparents, I learned something about life with her passing and knew I would miss her love and her kindnesses to me.

A Hardworking, Fun Summer

As school let out for the summer, I was excited to spend time helping Grandpa Wilberg on the ranch and attending several basketball camps. The most exciting, I think, was the Nike Camp at Princeton University. Not only did I play against some of the outstanding blue chip high school players in the country but also received classroom training, learning to develop better study habits. It was great, and I felt like I had somehow grown up a bit by the time the plane landed back in Salt Lake City.

Getting back to Castle Dale and to the ranch was pure exhilaration for me! While there has always been a lot of hard work to do, our family has always pitched in, making a fun time of it. The next few weeks were no exception as we branded calves, put up hay, moved cattle off the mountain, and in general built our muscles and worked our hearts out. And in between times, I worked out at our school—lifting weights, running, and having pickup games with the guys around town.

My Junior Year

As school began, I was excited to have Coach Jeffs as our new head basketball coach. As I mentioned, he had been an assistant coach the year before, and now he had taken over the program. I knew we would all miss Coach Nelson, but we were all eager to do a good job for our new coach, who had also grown up in Emery County and had participated in sports here.

In looking forward to the season, I was beginning to feel pressure that hadn't been there to this point. I had always created my own pressure to perform to my expectations, but now the pressure was coming from the press and from almost everyone I knew. I was the only member of our starting five to return, as the other four had graduated. So I knew it was up to me to provide leadership and to set the pace. I wasn't satisfied with our third-place ranking at state the year before, and I knew that unless we captured the crown, I never would be satisfied.

As for height, I was now 7'4" tall, wore a size 16 shoe, and thought that I had perhaps stopped growing. Because I hadn't ever experienced a growth spurt, I really hadn't gone through an awkward stage. To the contrary, I just found the floor getting further and further away from my eyes. Other than that and the fact that other players seemed to be getting smaller, I really didn't notice any great changes.

Our first five games went pretty much as expected, and even though we were working out the kinks with the new starting lineup, still we won each game and our confidence grew daily. But I felt this would be the case, since my classmates were now starters with me on the team and were gifted athletes. We had watched each other develop ever since our little league games, and although I had grown more in inches than the others, I certainly didn't see myself as any more talented. They were pure shooters and skilled in their positions, and playing with them was, in a word, *fun!*

Looking for our sixth straight win, we boarded the bus and drove over to our archrival, Richfield. Until this evening, I have never seen so much excitement for a rematch. As I've mentioned, Richfield beat us in the play-offs the year previous, and we were eager to measure up to our number one ranking in this game. We were both undefeated, and their star, Ryan Cuff, was really on a roll.

We were tied at the end of the first quarter, and it was an even game until the final seconds of the half. At that time, Ryan Stilson hit a long bomb from way behind the three-point line, so we led by four going into the locker room. The second half was pretty physical; in the final period alone, our team connected on 15 of 21 foul shots. We won the game, and I was flattered by Richfield's coach, Dwayne Peterson, as he made the following comments to the press:

"We didn't intend to put [Shawn] on the line as often as we did. He hit nine of his ten free throws. Shawn averages about 15 blocked shots per game. He didn't get that many against us, but he caused at least that many changes in our shots. Sometimes our players would go in and not shoot when he wasn't even near them."

The thing that pleased me was that I felt progress with my defense, and I knew that if I could maintain my intensity, I could have an impact on every team I played against.

We made our record 9-0 after winning our first region game against North Sevier. From the first basket, which I scored on a slam dunk after receiving an alleyoop pass from Ryan Stilson, to the final seconds, I was *wired*. I had eight dunks in the game and scored a career high 35 points. I was happy, too, for Lynn Tuttle, who had a slam dunk of his own, along with 15 points. It was a great way to begin region play!

One of the lessons this season continued to reinforce was how difficult it is to stay on top, once a team has been picked to win it all. This fact came forcefully to our minds the night we played the Manti Templars. We were going for our fifteenth straight win, and the Templars were also out to beat what many were billing as the top team in the state. They had entertained the same notion a month earlier, when we had played them the first time. But that night we broke a record by beating them 102-83. In the game that followed, we hit the century mark for the second time, this time against Gunnison. The final score on that game was 103-56. We knew this was hard for these teams to accept, but we had no idea that Manti would try to slow down our second game with them, as they did.

The first half was one of the most frustrating experiences of my life. In fact, by using a spread offense, Manti led 22-21 at halftime. Coach Jeffs and the other guys were just as anxious as I was, and yet we knew that patience was a new virtue we were trying to acquire, so we determined to just go back out and play our game.

As the second half began, I hit an eight-foot baseline jumper, followed by Steve Gordon's two free throws. Manti then scored in an effort to not get too far down, but I scored on an inside lay-up, which was followed by a spinning lay-up by Lynn Tuttle. All of a sudden we were in rhythm, and by being fed the ball, I scored the next eight points.

In all, I ended up scoring 28 points, and we won 64-43. As we looked back on the game, each of us knew what we had learned, and hopefully this game would help us during the final stretch of the season.

The last regular season game was against the Juab Wasps in Nephi. We had beaten them a month earlier in Castle Dale by a score of 80-49, and so we traveled over to their home crowd with quite a bit of confidence. They had also tried the spread slow-down offense on us, just as they had seen Manti do, but this tactic hadn't worked the first game, and we didn't think it would work in a rematch.

The game began quickly for me, as I made 11 points in the first eight minutes. These points proved to be half of what I would make in the entire game, but all of the guys were scoring whatever they threw toward the basket, so it got out of hand pretty early. The final score was 125-57, with our team winning by a record-setting 68 points. I felt badly for Juab, but all of our players got on the floor, and they just wanted to keep playing their hearts out. We scored 36 points in the final period, which was just awesome. Steve Gordon scored a season high 31 points, and I was happy for him and the others who played with a vengeance, getting ready for the region play-offs.

We had won eighteen games so far this season, and we wanted desperately to make it 24-0, after winning a first-ever state championship. For each of us, this seemed like an attainable goal. We had been ranked number one in the state since the first of the season, and we truly felt that we deserved this ranking.

Going to Region

The regional tournament was held at Snow College in Ephraim, just over the mountain to the west of us. We were glad it was so close, so more of our fans could make the trip. Fan support had become a trademark of our county, and as a team we fed from their enthusiasm more than I can express.

We won our first game quite handily, beating South Sevier 67-43 in the opening round of the tournament. The score didn't reflect the fact that our defense held South Sevier to just 19 first half points. I didn't do very well on offense, however, as I was held to just 12 points for the game. Still, I felt that my defense was improving, and I was satisfied with that.

In the second round, we again played Manti, a team from just seven miles to the south of Ephraim. They were the home team, for sure, but we hadn't been beaten all year, so we didn't let that bother us. I was more into the flow of offense in this game and ended up with 30 points. The final score was 69-57 in our favor, and according to Coach Jeffs, it was my best total game performance of the season. It was a great way to get psyched up for the championship game. I was personally hoping that would be against our archrivals, the Wildcats from Richfield. They had taken state the two previous years, and I wanted to beat them *badly!*

Richfield didn't disappoint me either, as they won their second round quite handily. This set up the region championship game, and there was total electricity throughout the city of Ephraim. As I mentioned earlier, Richfield had beaten us the year before, with Ryan Cuff having a career game. So we knew we were in for a battle, and the butterflies were really meddling inside my stomach.

As we all expected, the game was a real barn burner. With ten seconds to go in overtime, we were down one point but had the ball out of bounds. Coach gave us the play for the ball to come in to me, and for me to put it in the basket. The play worked perfectly, except that when I put it up, I threw up a brick. The ball just barely hit the backboard and didn't come anywhere near the basket. My heart sank, as I knew I had let our team down. But then I saw Lynn Tuttle out of the corner of my eye. He had boxed his man out and was grabbing the rebound. He was as cool as a cucumber, as he put up a nice jump shot that swished right through the net. Richfield got the ball with three seconds left, but they couldn't get it up the court to put it in.

So the game ended, and we won by one point, 67-66. Emery players and fans alike were yelling and screaming, and I was in a daze. Ryan Cuff had played a great game for Richfield, and I know he expected them to win. But it was our turn, and he was a good sport about it.

The days following the regional tournament were filled with more excitement and intensity than any I had previously known. We had overcome the Richfield jinx of the year before, and riding the wave of being crowned region champs gave us great momentum as we entered the state tournament.

Going to State

Our first game at state was with Morgan. We knew they were a good team, with very disciplined players, but we felt that we could beat them. It was a relief to get the first game jitters out of the way, as we won 75-59.

The semifinal game was against Hurricane, and even though I knew how important it was for me to keep out of foul trouble, I picked up my third foul only midway through the second quarter. I picked up a technical foul on the same call, so I spent the rest of the half on the bench. As the half ended, we held a 35-28 advantage. It wasn't a good omen, and as we went into the locker room, I was pretty fired up.

As the third quarter began, I still sat on the bench, with Coach Jeffs wanting to help me cool off so I would play without fouling when I returned to action. Finally, after what seemed like forever, Coach sent me back in. The frustration for me was that the refs were calling the second foul. The Hurricane defenders would foul me with their elbows, hitting me in the chest and gut, and then I'd retaliate and get called for it.

I joined our team on the floor, and before we knew it, Todd, Steve, and Chris had each scored three-pointers. Then I scored 18 of my 24 points, and the rest was history. We won 101-59 and were ready for the championship game. I was especially pleased with my free throw shooting, as I hit eight out of eight from the line. It was a great warm-up for the finale.

The championship game was with our archrival, Richfield, and my old nemesis, Ryan Cuff. As I mentioned in chapter 1, this game was described as perhaps the greatest prep basketball game played in the history of our state. Ryan Cuff had garnered MVP honors the year before, when Richfield had taken state. He had won this honor as a sophomore, which was an incredible feat. Now, with our winning it, the honor was passed on to me.

For our team, defeating two-time defending champions, Richfield, for the third time in the season, and the second time in as many weeks, was a thrilling way to leave 2-A competition. We knew we would be changed to 3-A competition in the fall and that we would rarely play them again. So, we savored our title and took a few days off before beginning spring sports.

My mom had kept stats on the team, and when the season ended, I was happy to learn that I had averaged 24 points, 8 rebounds, 7 blocked shots, 2 assists, and 2 steals. I was as satisfied with the assists and steals as I was with the other statistics, and I was even more pleased with how well the other players had done. Together, we had shown what could be accomplished with a group of dedicated, unselfish players. I'll give our coaching staff credit for instilling this attitude within us, and I'll give the entire team credit for pulling it off. It really had been a storybook season, and one that will forever hold special memories for me. An entire season without one loss!

Other Interests

In looking back through the previous pages, I almost appear one dimensional, which is anything but true. What I mean is that throughout the course of this school year, I had enjoyed serving as junior class president, performing in the school play, speaking at various functions around the state, being actively involved in the seminary program of the Church, and of course dating as many girls as I could. And this list doesn't include the constant pressure of work on the ranch, milking our cow, and doing the other chores that farm life provides.

Because athletics have been such a central focus of my life, part of my other interests included my academic endeavors. While I've never pretended to be the world's greatest brainchild, still I worked hard at my grades. Because of these efforts, and with the support of my parents and teachers, I was able to again be inducted into the National Honor Society. My classes weren't all easy, either. In addition to AP and honors classes, I took physics and intense subjects like that. Of course, my Uncle Duane was my physics instructor, and he was the best! He treated me like he did all the other kids, and because I took his class first thing in the morning, my senior year was action packed and intense from the first hour on.

From a spiritual standpoint, one of my greatest daily doses of learning was in seminary. During my four years of taking seminary, I had Brothers Seamons and Norton two years each. They were both outstanding teachers, and, even more important, they were true friends. They always encouraged me toward making correct choices and applying the scriptures to the here and now. There wasn't anything they wouldn't have done for me. In looking back, I'd have to say that these brethren taught me to like the scriptures and to enjoy reading them. Serving a mission, on the other hand, taught me to *love* the scriptures and to let them serve as a spiritual anchor in my life.

Dating

Let me share a few of my thoughts about dating. I won't use names of girls I dated in high school, simply because I don't want to offend anyone by leaving them out. Suffice it to say, the finest young ladies in the world grew up in my county, and we had some awesome times together.

On a more general note, our Church leaders have always counseled us to refrain from pairing off and dating until we were at least sixteen years old. Because my friends and I have been taught that the President of the Church is literally a prophet, seer, and revelator, I believe that what he has stated as revealed by the Lord for us should be adhered to. It seems like sound counsel to not begin the dating experience too early, so that relationships can be enjoyed without the intensity of heavy involvement at an early age. While growing up, I felt that by following the prophet with this counsel, I would be more apt to follow him in other directions of my life. I simply didn't want to become an adult who felt comfortable with picking and choosing which commandments, or directives, I would comply with. Although I'm far from perfect, my intentions have always been to exercise faith in Jesus by being obedient in all aspects of my life. Attending seminary each day in high school gave me the opportunity to ponder my level of commitment and to solidify the values that I wanted in my life.

On a lighter side of dating, one of the rare moments when being tall presented an obstacle was attending the junior prom. Imagine dancing with a girl at least two feet shorter than you, and you'll know how I felt. I decided to address this situation straight on and invited my date to dance on a chair. She graciously complied. This new way of dancing drew some strange looks and interesting stares at first but soon became accepted as being normal—at least for me.

From this evening on, if my date wasn't very tall, she would climb up on a chair, and we'd dance in that manner. It would always provide a good laugh, but the girls were always good sports about it.

Another aspect of my dating involved our cabin in Joe's Valley. Two or three couples would go out together, since we always thought we could have more fun when in a group setting. On many of these special occasions, Mom and Val LeRoy would fix us up a nice, hot meal and have it waiting to be served when we arrived at the cabin. Val and her husband, Drew, were the best of family friends, and their daughter, Shanae, who is about five years younger than me, has always treated me like I was her big brother. Dan and Breanne are the other two kids in the family, and they've always been there for us. In fact, some of our greatest family vacations have been with them.

Anyway, on our dates at the cabin, we'd eat, play group games of some kind, and then head down the canyon to the dance. Once there, we'd have our pictures taken, dance a few numbers, and enjoy being with the rest of the studentbody. Some out-of-towners have criticized our valley, saying there wasn't really anything to do for fun. But we were adventurous, and we created our own fun—never a dull moment, believe me!

This doesn't have to do with dating, really, but to illustrate what I'm talking about, my friends would sometimes tow a boat to school. Afterward, we'd take off and go water skiing, having the time of our lives. There are three lakes within fifteen miles of Castle Dale, and we'd make great use of them.

Another thing we'd do is drive down to the desert and ride three-wheelers all day. There was never a dull moment for any of us, and sometimes our folks would just shake their heads, wondering if we still lived at home or not.

Speaking of dating, one of our most favorite things to do was to go horseback riding. We'd make sure our dates had the tamest horses, unless we wanted to frighten them. Just kidding, of course. Anyway, we'd ride around the ranch or up in the foothills and have just a great time.

Baseball Season Begins

When our fertile, green valley had begun to blossom into spring, I was ready to begin baseball season. As I have mentioned, baseball has always been one of my favorite sports, and I have loved to pitch and play first base. Some people have been surprised when they've seen me in a baseball uniform. But the ones who know me, know I can play. Besides, it would have been a criminal offense to not give opposing pitchers such a giant strike zone to pitch to. It's really pretty hard to walk me, but after one guy did, his coach pulled him from the game. I learned afterward that the coach said, "If you can't throw strikes to a 7'5" guy, you can't throw strikes to anybody." He may have been kidding, but the pitcher who was taken out surely didn't think so. Actually, hitting the ball has always been easy for me, as Mom has constantly told me that I have good eye-hand coordination.

Without sharing the details of the season, let me just mention that I was able to lead the team with a .407 batting average. Blake Butler was the backbone of our team, though, and batted .385, while playing in all twenty of our games. I was only able to play in sixteen of the games, since I had basketball commitments that conflicted with the other four.

Special memories include our first game with Wasatch, where I made the first hit and run of the season for our team. In addition, I'll always remember the Mesquite tournament in Nevada, and hitting a three-run homer in one of those games. Even though we lost our first game in the state tournament against Lehi, it felt good to be enjoying one of my lifetime loves and to be part of such a great team. It's been such a different experience than basketball, where I have been the focus. Here I have just been another member of the team, and it has been totally pressure free and fun.

I had a great time pitching and got to do quite a bit of that on junior varsity. My coach taught me to throw sidearm, and with my long arms, it was like I was coming at the batter from third base.

Also, I have to thank the other guys on our team for never overthrowing me while I played on first. Of course, as Steve Gordon, our shortstop said, "If you overthrow Shawn, you'd better look for another sport. I would hate to be the one remembered for being the one who overthrew him." We all laughed when he said this, and again I appreciated the good humor of my friends and coaches and how well they dealt with my height.

Competing with the Soviets

Just days before my junior year came to a close, I had a once-in-a-lifetime opportunity to be on the Utah all-star team that would compete with the USSR Junior Olympic team that was touring the United States. I had always looked forward to playing against international competition, and this was the perfect chance to do so. My teammates consisted of Ryan Cuff, Ken Roberts, Jimmy Soto, Mark Durrant, Russell Larsen, and several others. Several of us had played together off and on for six years in the summer AAU league, and so we felt good about the two-week commitment of travel to Salt Lake City in order to jell as a worthy opponent.

When the game finally began, I was pretty tight. I could tell that Cuff was, as well, but Soto and Larsen picked up the slack, and when the final buzzer sounded, we had beaten the Soviet National Junior team 104-85. It was great, as almost six thousand fans turned out to support us. The Soviets had played four games in the previous five nights, though, and so we basically just wore them out. I only scored 12 points in the game, but I garnered 10 rebounds and 3 blocked shots, so I was satisfied. What I thought was especially great was how our team, made up of the best players in the state, were so unselfish in their play. For guys who were used to leading their teams, this game taught me a lot about cooperation and unselfishness. Also, I am hopeful that we were good hosts and that we demonstrated our clean-cut values to the Soviets. It was a game I'll always remember.

As summer arrived, I found myself gearing up to play on an all-star basketball team from Utah in the Reebock Slam-N-Jam Invitational Tournament. It was being held at Long Beach State, in California, and I traveled down with Coach Chuck Tebbs and the rest of the team. We also played in the Las Vegas BCI Tournament this summer, and played a good game together. These tournaments taught us a lot about playing against all-star quality opponents.

Using these tournaments as a springboard, my next trip was to the east coast, as I was invited to play in the Nike All-American Camp at Princeton University. It was great playing with guys who even now are beginning to play in the NBA.

When I returned from this trip, I found an unexpected letter waiting for me. It was from my friend, Danny Ainge. He had written from his home in Boston, and when I opened the letter, I found it to be a full six pages long. Among other things, Danny told me that Bob Ryan, a sportswriter for the *Boston Globe*, had written a two-page article on me, and evidently it was quite favorable. This article had triggered the letter from

Danny, and he gave me counsel about the things to consider in making a final decision about which college to attend. He gave me the critical questions I needed to answer for myself in selecting where I would attend, and then discussed how this choice would affect me for the rest of my life.

This unsolicited letter from one of the great basketball players in the NBA and who had been an All-American while playing for the Y had a great impact on me. In addition to providing me with perspective about my future with basketball, it also demonstrated how I wanted to treat others when I was down the road as far as Danny was. I wanted to still be a caring human being, and I knew that Danny Ainge was a great role model for me in this regard. I felt honored to have him for a friend.

My Senior Year

Leaving the ranching duties and the all-star basketball camps behind, I eagerly started high school for my last year. I was happy to have Brother Barry Norton again for my seminary teacher, and I felt comfortable with my progress toward serving a mission. He was always considerate of my time and treated me as though the Lord really did need me to serve others. Following his example, I tried to accommodate as many people as possible with whatever need they might have. I knew this year would be action packed, so instead of running again for class president, I accepted the invitation to run for vice president. My classmates supported me, and I was elected. Corinne Pugmire served this year as president, and it was great to work with her and the other officers—Karlene Mortensen, Chris Fish, Christine Greenwood, and Ellen Smith.

In mentioning the beginning of this school year, I must say that I found myself with a new sense of awareness of myself. Without knowing it, I had become a role model for my peers, as well as for younger children, and I didn't want to do anything that would disappoint them. For instance, one young boy turned twelve and was to be ordained a deacon in the Aaronic Priesthood. He invited me to assist in this ordination, and so I complied. I knew it meant a lot to him, and so it meant a lot to me, too. For those of you who aren't LDS, this meant that I would participate by putting my hands on his head, just as the ancient Apostles did for those they were ordaining, while his father acted as voice in bestowing a portion of God's power upon him. It is truly a sacred event.

After the ordination, my young friend's parents invited me to Sunday dinner, and it was great—both the dinner and being in their home. My philosophy on eating has always been to eat as often as I can wherever I can, and I think it paid off that Sunday, as the food was delicious. In fact, so was Mom's dinner when I got home.

Another young man flattered me by naming his cat, Shawn Bradley. He said he did this so he could tell his friends that he ate with "Shawn Bradley" every night. When I learned of this, I thought how lucky he was that it wasn't the *real* Shawn Bradley eating from their table; otherwise, they would have put out quite a bit of food. I really got a chuckle out of learning that.

Some of my happiest moments were in speaking to various youth groups. I loved seeing the innocent faith of children, and whenever I could, I would take the opportunity of mingling with them. One such occasion took place seven miles to the north of our ranch, in the small town of Huntington. I was visiting the Fourth Ward Primary, which consisted of children age three to eleven, as well as their leaders.

When I stood up to speak, I enjoyed the expressions on the faces of those kids. They kept looking me over, not sure if I was a giant, or something similar. Finally, smiling so as to put them at ease, I began: "Good morning. How is everybody today? I'm going to do a little talk on talents. Everybody has talents. You play soccer, football, basketball. Being a good friend is also a talent. Smiling is a talent. Being dependable is a talent. Heavenly Father wants us to discover our talents and work on them. I had to discover my talent and be willing to take the time to develop it. I have spent half my life practicing basketball. You have to work very hard to develop talents."

I could tell that I had their attention, and so I continued, becoming more specific: "I'm going to give you five points to remember: discover your talent; be willing to take the time to develop it; pray for help to Heavenly Father; practice, practice, practice; and lastly, share your talents."

I then closed my talk, and invited the children to ask questions. They weren't shy, either, and immediately a boy asked, "Are you a Boy Scout?"

"Yes," I answered, again smiling, "an Eagle Scout."

"How tall are you?" a girl asked, a deep furrow in her brow.

"I'm 7'5", almost. I hope I have my growth. I don't think I will grow any more. I weigh 211 pounds, and my shoes are size 16."

"How do you get to be so tall?" a second boy inquired, putting his hand over his head.

"Drink your milk and eat all your spinach."

"He had a growth *force*," another boy added, as they all laughed.

"How big were you when you were born?"

"I was twenty inches long, and weighed nine pounds fourteen ounces."

"Shawn," a girl asked, raising her hand but not waiting to be called on, "are you going to go on a mission?"

"Yes, I've always wanted to serve a two-year mission." That seemed to satisfy their questions, and so I again thanked them for the opportunity of speaking to them, and the meeting closed. Afterward, we went outside on the lawn, where they gathered around me for some photos. They were sitting on my lap, and swarming all around; and I'll have to say that life couldn't get any better than that. I drove my truck back home, sensing somehow that I was the real winner for having spent an hour with those kids. They were just great!

Deciding Early to Attend BYU

On Thursday morning, 14 September, I drove my truck up the highway toward our school, never suspecting the crowd of unknown cars that I found there. I had scheduled a news conference to announce my decision of where I would be playing college ball, and it seemed like the whole state had shown up for the event.

The past year or so had become a literal nightmare, as nearly every Division I basketball team in the country had contacted me, inviting me to come and play college ball for them. It was great for my ego—at least for a while. The enquiries became so constant, almost by the hour, that my folks and I were finding our heads swimming.

I had finally narrowed my choices down to Syracuse, UCLA, Arizona, North Carolina, Utah, Duke, and BYU. I finally announced this list, just so the other schools could concentrate their recruiting on players who really had a possibility of attending there. Then, finally, the day came when I knew deep within myself that I had to attend the Y. It was not a rational choice, really, although I was impressed with their developing basketball program. Rather it was a choice that was confirmed on my knees, in prayer, and that I couldn't deny was best for me. I'm not trying to paint myself as someone who prays about everything, even though the scriptures tell us this is what we should do. Even so, I *am* a young man who had previously inquired of the Lord about things in my life, and I knew the difference in my feelings when it was me answering my own prayers, or the Lord doing it. It was just a peaceful calm that stayed constant, never wavering. This is how I felt after deciding to attend the Y. Never once did my feelings change, and so I knew that in fairness to the other schools—before they took their recruiting trips to Castle Dale—I would contact them and let them know of my early commitment.

Once this was taken care of, and with the help of our principal, I scheduled the press conference for ten o'clock on the early fall morning of 14 September. With all the excitement in the air, he invited the entire studentbody to attend. The conference was to be held in our beautiful new school auditorium, and as the minutes drew near, I could almost feel the electricity in the air. Finally, after being introduced, and with my mom and dad standing on each side of me, I smiled, swallowed hard, and spoke.

"Ladies and gentlemen of the press," I began slowly, "welcome to Emery County. It's a real honor for me to stand in front of you today. I'm grateful for this opportunity. I appreciate all the effort you made in coming here.

"Although it's still early in the season for deciding which college I will be attending, I have found a school I want to go to, and one which will meet all my needs for several years to come. This decision does not come lightly nor prematurely, as it has been at least a four-year process in developing. But it is the right decision for me, and I feel privileged even to be able to make it.

"So, come November's national letter of intent signing time, I will sign with Brigham Young University." At that moment, I was quite startled when the crowd stood and cheered—and almost lifted the roof off our auditorium. It was sheer madness. Finally, after what seemed like forever, they calmed down, and I continued.

"This decision does not in any way detract from the high class academic and athletic programs of other colleges which were recruiting me and how incredibly well I was treated by all of their coaching staffs. I had a wonderful time being able to associate with men of such caliber, and I'm grateful to all of them. But now I'm moving on, and I'm going to dedicate myself to the special coaching staff at BYU—Coaches Reid, Engel, and Bradley—whom I deeply respect. From this point forward, I will add to my Emery colors of black and gold the color of BYU blue and wear it proudly. Thank you."

Well, that was the announcement, and I surely felt good making it. In a way, I felt as though a load of bricks had been lifted from my shoulders. Over one hundred and twenty colleges had been recruiting me, and after narrowing it down, I knew deep down that the Y was where I should go. I actually made the decision the previous Monday night, but my folks advised me to sleep on it and see how I felt the next morning.

When I did feel the same, I shared my feelings with Mom, and she was excited I would be playing close enough for them to see the games. I then called Dad at the Emery County Clinic where he works and told him. He was also elated and relieved, and told me he felt I had made the right decision. I then called Coach Reid, to let him know, but he was busy, and it wasn't until later in the day that he called back and received the news.

When I finally visited with Coach Reid, his entire office staff went crazy on the other end of the line. I was the first recruit he would sign as head coach, and this meant a lot to him. He assured me that the folks at the Y would assist me in whatever way they could as I attempted to make the transition to college ball and being away from home. I also felt good that I had made the announcement so that other schools could concentrate their recruiting energies on more likely candidates. It was tempting to be wined and dined by them and to visit their campuses, but I knew that I couldn't compromise my integrity by allowing it to play itself out. It just wouldn't have been right. Now, with all the pressure off, I felt great, and went to sleep that night with more peace of mind than I had known for months.

Making the Golf Team

After making the decision to attend the Y, I settled into a more normal lifestyle than I had known for over two years. The phone quieted down, the interviews lagged off, and I looked forward to a great school year. Part of my excitement at this time was because of making our school's golf team. It was the first year we had competed in golf, and I really wanted to be a part of it. I took a little ribbing when I made the team, since my uncle, Duane Merrell, was the coach. But I took it in stride, as I had learned to play the links here in the valley, as well as in Price, and I felt I could make a contribution. Because I wanted to play to my potential, Coach Rick Majerus of the University of Utah helped find me a set of extra-long clubs to play with. I actually bought them from former Wyoming and then NBA player, seven-foot Chris Engler. They're not quite as long as I would like, but they've been great. My low score for nine holes was a 42, and I was pretty excited to record it.

As the golf season concluded, I was surprised and happy to learn that I had played the lowest round on our squad, even though I wasn't one of the regularly low scorers. We had a great time, though, and I really appreciated the therapy of golfing, knowing that in just a few weeks I would be back in the pressure cooker of basketball.

Working at Tracy's Service Station

In addition to playing golf, my schedule allowed me time to work at Tracy's gas station after school. President Tracy Jeffs, who was a member of our stake presidency, offered me a job since I had spent a lot of time at the station the previous two years. I had been restoring the old GMC pickup that my uncle

Duane had given me, and Tracy and I had become great
friends. But now he said that I could get a regular paycheck for
my hours worked, or I could trade truck parts for my labor.

This proposition was pretty exciting, and before I knew it I
was pumping gas, repairing tires, doing lube jobs, and in general becoming acquainted with servicing cars. The funniest (or
most frustrating) moments were whenever I had a car up on
the lift so that I could lube it or drain the oil. I had to put on
knee pads, then kneel down and walk under the car on my
knees. I was simply too tall to stand up and work.

I might add that for the previous two years I had been able
to work on my truck, beginning with installing new brake
shoes. That task alone took me two days, and with the truck
wheels torn down, I had driven my bike the three miles from
Tracy's to my home. But I had done that for years, and so it
was really no big deal. I also replaced the muffler, shocks, and
other things; so my truck was becoming quite a machine.

One Saturday, while Tracy and I were masking off my truck
so I could paint it, we had a conversation that I'll always
remember.

"You know, Shawn," Tracy began, "I've known you almost
all of your life, and I've been measuring pretty much every one
of your footsteps."

"Excuse me? I . . . uh, I'm not sure I follow you. . . ."

"Well, then," Tracy continued, setting the tape down on the
hood, "let me be more direct. You've always been tall for your
age, and I suppose your size has mostly been a blessing for you.
With the exception, of course, of times like last summer at
youth conference, when you wanted me to find you some roller
skates big enough to fit your size sixteens."

"Yeah," I laughed, "that was frustrating not being able to
get out on the rink like all the others."

"What you don't know, Shawn, is what happened the next
day when Mike Smith, from BYU's basketball team, came and
spoke. After he finished speaking, I went up to him, as you
asked me to, and told him that you were at the conference."

"Oh, I remember that, all right. He was cool."

"Well, what you don't know, Shawn, is that when I told him
you wanted to meet him, his reply was, 'I would die to meet
Shawn!' It was a privilege for *him* to meet you, even though you

thought of it as just the opposite. That's the impact you're having on people, Shawn, and I know you're humbled by it.

"Anyway," Tracy continued, "like most folks, I've enjoyed watching you grow. But I've also enjoyed watching your personality develop. For some time now, I have felt that you have been sent to earth for a different purpose, and that not only in height, but in stature, you're a notch above the rest of us. You're a lot like Joseph Smith, Shawn. Folks loved to just be around him and to partake of his great spirit. You have that same spirit, Shawn, and you need to guard it so you don't lose it."

I smiled awkwardly, uncomfortable with Tracy's words of praise and yet sensing that he was about to tell me something that I should give heed to.

"Several years ago," he added, "while you were passing the sacrament to the congregation at Church, it occurred to me that you had an unusual gift of interacting with others. As I just said, you're a people person, Shawn, and I wouldn't be surprised if one day you won't become a significant role model by the message that you share."

Not knowing how to respond, I simply leaned against the truck and looked down at Tracy, allowing him to continue.

"Oh, you'll be a great missionary, Shawn, wherever it is the Lord sends you. But I wouldn't be surprised if your two-year mission is simply one of preparation . . . and that the Lord will then use you to teach others how life ought to be lived."

"Those are pretty tall words you're using, Tracy. I just hope I don't disappoint the Lord—or anyone else, for that matter."

"I have a feeling that you won't," Tracy concluded. "From where I stand, you're walking along your appointed path with pretty sure footing, and I suspect things will work out like they're supposed to. Someone asked me the other day what your hallmark qualities were, and in addition to your work ethic, I told them honesty and integrity. Those are pretty good foundation blocks for all of us, and I think they'll fare you well as you prepare for what lies ahead in your life."

At that moment, someone came into the station and asked for Tracy's assistance. He left to help, and for a long time after our conversation ended, my mind kept rehearsing what he had said. It made me especially happy that he had recognized my desire to be honest. But I had known no other way, and so I didn't see it as something I should have false pride about.

I also knew that somehow what Tracy said about my future was true. I also knew that I made mistakes every day of my life, and it concerned me that my actions might cause someone else to stumble on their path. It was truly food for thought.

Bagging My First Buck

Although in previous years friends had taken me out hunting, even before I was old enough to carry a rifle, I finally had the opportunity to go out and test my own shooting skills. Our family friend, Drew LeRoy, invited me to go. We left home in the predawn hours on the first morning of the hunt, and I was totally psyched. We then drove up to Horn Mountain, above Joe's Valley, and arrived while it was still dark. Finally, when the sun began to rise, it was one of the most awesome sights I've ever seen. The morning rays coming from the east and flooding the changing leaves of fall were just spectacular!

As we loaded our rifles and started to walk away from the truck, we saw some really fresh tracks, and our hearts started pounding. We began following them, and about a mile up the side of the mountain, we could tell where they were going. So we backtracked to the truck and drove it around the rim to where we thought they would be.

Sure enough, as we got out of the truck and walked to the edge of the clearing, we looked down and spotted a buck and a doe, prancing along. Drew shot first—and missed. Then I did the same. He then shot and missed the second time, and by then I was calmed down, and I shot and hit the buck right in the rib cage. I wasn't sure that I'd hit him, though, and after Drew shot a third time, both deer ran into some trees out of our line of fire.

We saw the doe come out of the other side of the stand of trees, and I thought they had either split and would join back up later on or that one of us had maybe hit the buck. So I took off after the doe, and Drew worked his way down into the trees. After I'd gone about a mile and a half, I thought I had made a mistake, so I doubled back to find Drew. I wasn't sure I could get off the mountain alone, and I knew he could.

When I finally arrived back in the trees, Drew was up to his elbows in blood, cleaning the buck that I had shot. I didn't believe I had shot it at first, but Drew said that his bullet couldn't have made the same entry and exit markings that mine had done and that I had definitely bagged my first deer. He had basically finished cleaning it by that time, and since it was a huge 20″ two-point, we had to drag it about two hundred yards up the side of the mountain toward the truck. It actually took us the rest of the day to get that big carcass off the mountain, but by the time we got home, I was as proud as any guy in Emery County.

Basketball Season, at Last

While I enjoyed going to the football games and being supportive of my friends on the team, I was relieved when the weeks of fall had passed and it was time for basketball season to begin.

After such a storybook junior year, with our first state championship, I knew I would be hard-pressed to make my senior year measure up. We had only lost two starters, Todd Huntington and Lynn Tuttle, from last year's squad, so we felt pretty confident that we could repeat as state champs. This became our goal, right from day one. Other than myself, we had two other starters back—Steven Gordon and Ryan Stilson—as well as Chris Wilson, who had come off the bench and played great.

The other starters—namely Ryan Stilson, Chris Wilson, Cody Allred, and Steve Gordon—gathered around me, and we felt a bond of unity that is difficult to describe. I was especially proud of Cody, our point guard. He had been a great wrestler our sophomore year, but Coach knew that Todd Huntington would need to be replaced our senior year, so he brought Cody onto the team as a junior. As a result, Cody worked his heart out to catch up with the rest of the team. He became so good as point guard that the ball seemed at times simply an extension of his hands. Steve Gordon, the other guard, knew how to shoot the ball. He was one of the purest three-point shooters I had known, even under pressure, as winning the championship the year before had shown.

Even though Steve and Cody were small in size, they were giants in my eyes. I knew Ryan and Chris felt the same way, and we were proud to be playing with them. Chris, who was 6'4", was our team "psycho" and played with a vengeance. He just did what he had to to get the job done. Ryan was about the same height as Chris and was our team "horse." I knew he would play every second with total intensity and could do it all. Coming off the bench, we had Jason Nelson, our former coach's son, along with Scott Chynoweth and Rob Wagoner. Even though they didn't share equal playing time during the games, they gave 110 percent in every practice and made our team realize its potential. They were great teammates and true friends.

I had an experience at the beginning of the season that is funny looking back on it, although at the time I took a lot of ribbing from my teammates. While working at the station, Tracy and I had changed the camshaft in my pickup, and I had gotten urethane glue all over my hands. It felt a little strange playing basketball with all of that glue on my hands, but maybe it helped me hold onto the ball a little better. As I said, my teammates teased me about it, but I had a new camshaft that had sealed up just right, so I didn't mind.

As a way to tip off the season, the high school athletic association decided to stage a rematch between our team and Richfield, only this time in the Marriott Center at Brigham Young University. We thought this would be great, especially since we had beaten Richfield three out of three times our junior year. Ryan Cuff was also back as a senior, and so it shaped up to be the rubber match of our careers.

Cuff of Richfield started off fast, giving them the early lead. But we came back, and by half we led 37-30. They also came back, though, and the final quarter was right out of the wild, wild west. The players on both teams spent as much time on our faces as we did playing. In the last seconds we were up by four points, but Cuff hit a shot at the buzzer, cutting our margin of victory to two, 55-53. It wasn't a game of finesse by any means, but I was able to get 21 points for Emery. We had good balance in scoring, too, with Stilson getting 11 points and Gordon getting 10. On the other hand, Cuff for Richfield put in 35 points and had quite a few assists. He was a machine, and I was happy for his success. I just hoped he would sign to play at the Y also, and then we could combine our energies for the same team.

Our win meant that of the six times we played Richfield in my three years, we had won the last five. I just hoped it would prove to be a good omen for our season!

The Senior Ball—with Crutches

As the preseason continued, we won the next four games quite handily. While things were going great on the hardcourt, my duties as vice president of our class included making preparations for our senior ball. I invited a friend, Sheri Burnett, from Salt Lake City, and we knew it would be a date to remember. We were doubling with my friend, Billy Wright, and his date, Amy Tuttle, and we planned on showing the girls the time of their lives. Our plans were to start the evening by riding horses to an old abandoned pioneer cabin in the desert, eat dinner, and afterwards go to the dance.

Everything began as planned, but as we were riding our horses toward the cabin, my horse suddenly went crazy. Sheri and I were riding together and stopped for a minute to let Bill and Amy catch up with us. I don't know what happened next, but maybe my horse just didn't want to stand there with us on top, for before we knew what was happening, he threw his head back and hit me in the forehead. He then started running backward, finally tripping and falling down. Horses just aren't made to run backward! Anyway, we were thrown off, with my horse landing on top of me. He quickly jumped up and started to run, but before I could yank my foot out of the stirrup, I was dragged along for twenty to thirty yards.

I must have sat there for ten minutes before finally getting up to see if I could walk. My right knee was badly bruised, and I could tell that my kneecap ligaments had been strained. I limped around some, but did that ever hurt!

Bill and Amy went for some help, and before long my brother, Justin, drove the truck up to get me. Soon I was down in Castle Dale, having X rays in the medical center. I didn't want to ruin the evening completely, though, as I knew Sheri had driven a long ways to attend the dance, so with a brace and on crutches, I was released by the doctors to attend the dance.

Well, we didn't do much dancing, I assure you, but I was able to do my duties of introducing the winners of the senior royalty, which consoled me somewhat. I hadn't been injured like this before, and the only thing I could think of was how such a fluke injury might put all my basketball playing days behind me. At any rate, the dance was great, and I promised Sheri that we would take a rain check on dinner at the old cabin.

Our next game, with Payson, was the next week, and although my knee was still sore, I was able to play without much problem. It ended with a seven-point victory for us, 67-60, and from this game on we knew that we couldn't let down our guard with anyone. Each of our opponents thought of their game with us as a "career" opportunity, since we were again ranked first in the state—the team to beat.

A Road Trip to St. Louis

With a preseason record of 6-0, we had the opportunity to take the first of two eastern road trips and play in high school tournaments with other teams that had also been invited to participate. This first tourney, with a field of twelve teams from throughout the country, was held in St. Louis, Missouri. In our first game, we beat a good St. Louis team 84-47, and I was able to score 20 points, grab 16 rebounds, and block 9 shots. Steve Gordon took top scoring honors, however, with 22 points. He proved once again that his three-point shooting wasn't a fluke the year before, as he continued to hit the bomb from outside.

Our other games followed the course of the first, and before we knew it, we had won the tournament and were flying home with our championship trophy.

A Second Trip, This Time to North Carolina

Traveling to Raleigh, North Carolina, was a Christmas holiday that will be hard to match. In the first round against a Maryland team, we won 70-54. What we weren't prepared for was the caliber of the second team, from Memphis, Tennessee. They beat us 78-68 and gave us a good serving of humble pie. The last night we played against the hometown team from

Durham, and they beat us even further, by a score of 66-47. It was great playing against Anfernee Hardaway, Rodney Rogers, and other all-star players, but we limped back into Castle Dale having suffered our first two defeats in two seasons. Even so, we felt that we had learned a lot from such outstanding competition and knew that we could use the experience as a springboard for the rest of the season.

Region Ball Begins

After returning from North Carolina, we were all eager to get into region play and see how it was among the larger 3-A schools. What none of us had anticipated was the notoriety we would receive wherever we went. I guess it was a combination of people never having seen a seven-foot-five-inch ball player before, as well as the fact that we were an upstart bunch of kids from Emery County, who were state champions, but only in the 2-A bracket. Whatever it was, the adrenaline sure was pumping wherever we traveled.

To illustrate, when we went to Roosevelt and played Union High, we arrived at three in the afternoon. Our junior varsity team traveled with us, of course, and their game began a half hour later. So, here it was four hours before tip-off of our varsity game, and a crowd of between two and three hundred fans were already lined up for tickets. They knew there wouldn't be any seats left if they came in the evening, so they were there for about six hours in anticipation of some good competition. And of course we tried not to disappoint them—we cleaned their plow by a score of 117-87. It was an offensive show from start to finish, and a game I'll always remember.

But this experience was typical of wherever we went. Coach Jeffs talked to us about it and called my height a sideshow that we would just have to deal with, without becoming distracted by it. My teammates were the greatest, too, as they would make room for the television cameras, as well as the fans. Oh, they'd ham it up by waving at the cameras, like teenagers do, but basically their lack of jealousy and their support made it possible for me to get through it without losing my sanity.

As for me, I was honored by the interest and respect people showed me, and I made every effort to give them my autograph without losing sight of the fact that we were a team, and playing as a team was the only way we could accomplish our goals. I knew the Lord had given me the gift of size and the ability to play with coordination, and I couldn't take credit for that.

Even more than this, I was just happy to be one of the guys on our team. Although we were far from being perfect, we did share the same values, and so it wasn't hard to have good, clean fun while not getting caught up in the idea that we were better than others. Coach Jeffs once told me that the tallest men remained humble, and I think that as a team, we could all say that regardless of our height in inches, or our level of skill, we have helped each other stand tall and thus enjoy a measure of humility.

Our last two regular season games were against Wasatch High, from Heber. We won the first by a score of 59-50, and the second 91-77. What we hadn't anticipated was that we would also be playing them in our sole regional game, making them our opponents for three consecutive weeks! I figured they didn't want to play us any more than we wanted to play them, but we poured it on at region, winning that by 18 points, 81-63. This was a crazy way for us to prepare for the state 3-A tournament, but we were still on a roll and hadn't lost a game in Utah for the second season in a row.

The State 3-A Tournament

We were playing in the 3-A bracket for the first year, and the state tournament was held in Ogden at the Dee Events Center. Our first opponent was Dixie High School, from St. George. They were one of the teams that had further to drive than we did, but we knew they would come ready to play, so we didn't take them for granted. The 3-A tournament, as opposed to the three-game format for 2-A, was a four-game single-elimination tournament. We had to beat Dixie in order to reach the quarterfinals, and we knew we couldn't stub our toes in our first-ever 3-A tournament game.

As it turned out, we had a relatively easy time of it with Dixie. The final score was 73-35, and our confidence level was soaring. We found out something during that game, and that was how much time was spent by our opponents in trying to figure out how to play against a seven-and-a-half foot center. They hadn't had this experience before, and so we were well on our way to victory before they figured out how to guard me.

The quarterfinal game was next, against the Box Elder Bees from the northern part of the state. They seemed a little better prepared than was Dixie and played us tough. We finally came out victorious, though, with a final score of 65-43. After the game, Coach Jeffs reminded us that it was too early to celebrate and that we still had two games left to achieve the goal we had set at the first of the season. So we sobered up, got a good night's sleep, and prepared for the game with Jordan two nights later.

After what seemed like forever, Friday night finally arrived, bringing with it our matchup with the Jordan Beetdiggers from Salt Lake County. They were city boys and looked pretty sharp during warm-ups, but we were a smooth-oiled machine by this time, and so we weren't intimidated. The final score of this game was 68-39, with our team again being the victors. It seemed impossible, especially with all the distractions, but here we were again, only this time in the larger 3-A bracket, vying for the state championship.

For the championship, we found ourselves staring into the eyes of the hometown team, Ogden High. We knew they had worked hard to get to this point and that the game would be hard fought. But we also knew that we had the psychological edge, coming in as former state champs and as the number one—ranked team in the state.

This time, as we warmed up, I wasn't nauseous as the year before, but I still had plenty of butterflies. I knew we could win, though, if we kept our focus, and before I knew it, the game had begun. The greatest advantage we had was that they had not played us before and so weren't used to compensating for my size in the middle.

The game was hard fought, but never as close and tense as the previous year with Richfield. We won quite easily, by a score of 84-71, garnering our second state championship in a row. Where the previous championship was filled with ecstacy and elation, this one was filled with relief. There had been so much pressure on us throughout the season, as everyone expected us to repeat. Now that we had done just that, without losing our focus, I felt like our rural Utah farm boy label had been enhanced, as we had proven ourselves with the larger 3-A competition from the cities. When we returned home, we received another police escort into town, but this time we came from the north, since the tournament had been held in Ogden.

As the season ended, our record stood at 22-2, with our only two losses being in the North Carolina tournament. In reflecting on my high school career, I realized that counting the two losses at the end of my sophomore season, our record for the past three years stood at 64-4.

During my final season as a Spartan, I averaged 26 points, 13 rebounds, and 9 blocked shots. As mentioned, my high-scoring game garnered me 39 points. My high rebound total for one game stood at 18, and during one game I blocked 16 shots. I was fortunate to have averaged 58 percent of my field goals during my high school career and to make 71 percent of my free throws. Those were satisfying stats for me, and I felt that I could now move on to the next level, that of collegiate competition.

The thing that I'll always remember about that season is how we all worked together, never thinking that one of us was more important than another. I have to give Coach Jeffs and Coach Jones credit for instilling this attitude of unselfishness in us. I will especially remember the teammates who didn't see a lot of playing time during these years, but who worked their hearts out in practice and gave the rest of us the practice competition we needed to win our back-to-back state championships.

The other thing I'll remember is how unified we were as a studentbody. The students and faculty shared in the excitement and recognition that Emery County had received. And I want to mention the folks who lived in the surrounding towns. They were great, and treated us like heroes!

Personally, I was sad to know that I had played my last game as a Spartan. But even more, I was relieved that the overwhelming pressure of winning a second state championship was over and that some of the spotlight with press conferences and others could slow down. I was pleased to have been a spokesman for my teammates, and yet the constant ringing of the phone and visits by the press had taken its toll on our family. Now I could relax, enjoy the final months of high school, and then prepare for my future as a Cougar at BYU.

Speaking of the Y, throughout the winter I had been invited to a couple of their home basketball games, and they'd been great. It had been fun going into the Marriott Center, too, knowing that I would be playing in a Cougar uniform in just a few short months. I'd had fun with my height, too, even though it had been difficult sitting down without inconveniencing people sitting behind me. In fact, it became such a big thing that in the *Cougar Illustrated* annual "Best and Worst Awards," I won the "Worst Seat in the House" award. As it stated, it was "for the seat in the VIP section, right behind 7-foot-5 recruit Shawn Bradley." They were good sports, though, and I tried to slide forward in my seat so they could see the game.

All-Star Tournaments

Weeks after my teammates had checked in their uniforms, I found myself traveling with my family to the Las Vegas AAU tournament in Nevada. I was part of the Utah all-star team, along with Ryan Cuff of Richfield, Ken Roberts of Bingham, and others.

On 16 May, we found our team assembling for an all-star game to be played in Salt Lake City at the Huntsman Special Events Center. We were playing the Russian Junior Olympic team, and were we ever psyched!

Perhaps the most exciting all-star tournament for me to attend was the 13th annual McDonald's All-American game in Indianapolis, Indiana. It was an East-West contest, and so naturally I was on the West team, with Eric Montross from Indiana. I knew we would share playing time, but that didn't matter since our main goal was to serve as role models to the less fortunate kids at the Ronald McDonald House. It felt great helping them smile, and one little seven-year-old named Walter Parker really captured my heart.

During this weekend I learned about Hoosier Hysteria. I had heard the words, but being there and seeing the excitement of the fans was something else. Basketball is on the rise in Utah, but the fans aren't anything like these people.

The game was pretty even throughout most of the contest, but they pulled ahead in the final two minutes, and we ended up losing 115-104. I only played 16 minutes but felt good about scoring 12 points, with 10 rebounds and 6 blocks. When I heard the announcer call out my name as winning the MVP award for the West team, I was elated. I had worked hard all week. A guard, Khalid Reeves of Queens, New York, who was on his way to play for Arizona, won MVP for the East squad, and he really won the game for them in the closing minutes.

While back East, I was also honored to have played in the All-Star Capitol Classic, again sponsored by McDonald's, in Washington, D.C. Ken Roberts was there with me, and we even visited President Bush at the White House. President Bush autographed my shoe for me and seemed very genuine while visiting with the team.

Senior Honors Assembly

One of our school's great traditions has been to host an assembly at the conclusion of each school year so that the seniors could receive recognition for the accomplishments they had made. On this year's program, Steve Gordon and Cody Allred were named Outstanding Male Athletes. I was excited for them in receiving this distinction, as they had spent literally thousands of hours in several sports over their high school careers.

I was named MVP for our basketball team and received all-state and other honors. The most memorable moment, however, was when Coach Jeffs invited me to the podium and announced that they were retiring my jersey—number 45. They had both of my jerseys framed and gave me the road jersey, while keeping the white home jersey for the school. It was a great moment for my family, and one that I will long remember.

Graduating—at Last

As graduation day approached, my friends and I found ourselves signing yearbooks, spinning our wheels up to Joe's Valley, and in general having a blast. We knew these were moments that could never be recaptured, and we were focussed on living them to their fullest! Still, I settled down long enough to complete my finals and to complete my assignments as class officer.

When graduation day arrived, my emotions went from one extreme to another. First, I was elated that I had successfully completed such a storybook high school career. Then I would become saddened to think that I would never again be walking the halls of Emery High School with my friends. I knew I was ready to leave home and to attend college, but I still found myself becoming nostalgic with the fact that never again would I be here as a student and athlete, though I'd always have my friends.

As summer began, our family took our first-ever trip to Lake Powell. It was so awesome, and since I had learned to slalom water ski, I had the time of my life. Justin and Tasha skied well too, and even Adrianne and Dad were able to get up on one ski. My mom is the only one who didn't slalom, even though she had a great time water skiing the easy way. Drew and Val LeRoy and their three kids took us down, and we stayed on their houseboat at Hanson Creek, skiing to our heart's content. It was on this trip that I became addicted to Lake Powell.

The weather was so hot that we had to stay in the water just to keep cool. We also went sightseeing on the lake and enjoyed exploring different canyons that had become part of the 100-plus-mile long lake. I knew this was a week to enjoy myself, since I would soon be busy with basketball camps, ranching, and getting ready for college. My life was changing rapidly, and I just hoped that I had the stamina to respond to the demands placed upon me, but every prior year had better prepared me for life in the fast lane.

At eight months old I posed with Mom and Dad for this family Christmas card while we were living in Zweibruecken, Germany.

My very first Christmas present was a new basketball.

At age two, dressed in German Lederhosen.

My best friend, Apache.

This photograph with Grandpa Wilberg was taken at our family's cabin in Joe's Valley when I was five.

Branding cattle was one of the many ranching chores I learned to do with Grandpa.

Playing baseball for the Castle Dale Cougars was pretty much my spring activity during my grade school years.

At ten years old and just under six feet tall, I won the 4-H one-on-one basketball state competition.

I played quarterback for the Colts in Little League football. In this team picture I'm standing in the back row by myself.

Mom, Tasha, Justin, Adrianne, Dad, me, and Smokey (our dog)
in front of our Castle Dale home in 1984.

Cutting down the net after our 68–65
victory over the Canyon View Cougars
in the 1987 junior high league
championship game.

Ninth grade graduation with best
friend, Greg Huntington.

One of the "honors" of being sophomore class president at Emery County High was to ride on the homecoming float.

Throughout my junior year the catalogs I accumulated from nearly every Division I university literally covered my bed.

*1989 state tournament play
against the Morgan High Trojans.*

*Playing against high school
archrivals, the Richfield Wildcats.*
Photo courtesy of Ravell Call

*Emery County High's final year of 2-A basketball competition ended with
a thrilling 84–83 victory over Richfield for the state championship.*

*Playing against the USSR Junior Olympic team as a member of the 1989
Utah all-stars was an unforgettable experience.*

*I made the golf team during my
senior year. My game improved
after Coach Rick Majerus of the
University of Utah helped me
find these extra-long clubs to
play with.*

*Dancing with a girl at least two feet shorter
than you presents some real challenges.*
Photo courtesy of Ravell Call

This will always be my "home" court, behind our house in Castle Dale.
Photo courtesy of Budd Symes

Receiving the MVP award for the West team (along with Khalid Reeves as MVP for the East team) from John Wooden following the 13th annual McDonald's All-American game.

The 1990 Spartan basketball team seniors—me, Rob Wagoner, Cody Allred, Steven Gordon, Scott Chynoweth, Ryan Stilson, Chris Wilson, and Jason Nelson.

Major college ball was a
quantum leap upward from
high school. It was an
incredible season, with a WAC
tournament championship and
an NCAA post-season berth.

Despite a midseason slump, I was
able to set a new NCAA freshman
season blocked-shot record with
177 blocked shots.

Photos courtesy of Mark Philbrick

This statue of Brigham Young stands in the center of the
BYU campus. I'm proud to be an alumnus of such an
outstanding school and basketball program.

Saying good-bye to my family at the airport before flying to Australia to serve my mission.

As my mission came to an end I knew that I could never walk taller than I did as a Mormon missionary in Sydney, Australia.

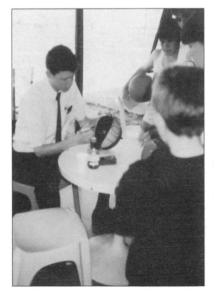

There were constant opportunities to explain my basketball career that I'd put on hold and why I had chosen to serve a mission.

Lake Powell was the perfect place to escape the pressures of the media and the approaching NBA draft.

NBA commissioner David Stern congratulating me on being drafted by the Philadelphia 76ers.

September 25, 1993—
My temple marriage to
Annette Evertsen was my
greatest moment ever.

Photos courtesy of Dale P. Hansen, Mar Del Photography

I'm elated to be a Philadelphia 76er, but I'm still just a twenty-one-year-old farm kid from central Utah who happens to love basketball.

Photo courtesy of the Philadelphia 76ers

5

A Quantum Leap into College

To Provo in My GMC

As at last I finished packing and headed north toward Provo and BYU, I felt a little of myself dying. I knew I would always go back to Castle Dale and that it was my home, but never again would I be there enjoying the carefree life of a teenager. Nor would the friendships be the same. The adults and youth of Emery County had given me so much, and I knew the only way I could repay them was to be true to myself and to give 100 percent to whatever my life's profession would provide. I knew that more than almost anything, I wanted to become an impact player in the NBA. I say *almost,* because more than anything I wanted to serve the Lord on a mission and then to marry for eternity in one of His holy temples.

For now, though, I wanted to get settled in at the Y and get a good start as a first-semester freshman. I also wanted to become acquainted with the basketball players and coaches and to make the adjustment to a college basketball program. I was glad that Ryan Cuff, of Richfield, and Ken Roberts, of Bingham, were both coming to the Y, although Ryan would serve his mission before playing his freshman year of eligibility. I was also proud to be part of a team that valued missions and gospel standards as I did. I knew I was no more perfect than they, and yet we shared a value system that would provide support for each of us.

Two hours after leaving home, I pulled my truck to a stop in front of John Hall, my new on-campus home at BYU. My folks had followed me in their van, bringing what I couldn't carry in the pickup. We moved in, then went out for lunch. After that, we returned to the dorm, and I met Ken Roberts, my high school all-star teammate, who had been assigned as my roommate. My folks finally returned home, leaving me on my own as an excited new Cougar. As I became acquainted with campus, my first interest was the cafeteria. Along with the other team members, we loved the food at the Cannon Center and were always given all we could eat. College life looked good, and even though school hadn't started, I knew I was in for a wild ride my freshman year. The girls were awesome and plentiful, and with my restored blue-with-pink-pinstriping GMC, I was in fat city!

The Coach and Team

I was pretty psyched to get to know the coaches at the Y. The head coach, Roger Reid, was in his second season as head coach and had won the Western Athletic Conference title the year before with a 21-9 rookie season record. Tony Ingle, one of the assistants, had come from the Deep South the year before and had a great sense of humor and terrific coaching skills. The other full-time assistant was Charles Bradley, who came to BYU from Wyoming, with an interim stay at San Diego State. He had played pro ball with the Boston Celtics and Seattle Supersonics, and I especially looked forward to his player-coach perspective of the game.

These men had a work ethic that I knew I could live with, and since our high school team had developed championship perspective, that part of my transition into college ball would be quite easy. By the time the season was on us, I had learned to respect each coach in his own way, and I felt that this respect was mutual. They assured me that I could make an immediate contribution to the team, and so I began my college career with a *starter's mentality*.

I was especially looking forward to playing with senior Steve

Schreiner. He had played on the national championship team at Dixie College before serving a mission for the Church in Japan. Steve was a true team leader, and I learned a lot from him, even before the season began.

Others figuring to start were Nathan Call, a returned missionary from Bolivia, and Ken Roberts, my friend and new roommate. Also figuring in were Jared Miller, a transfer from Ricks, and Mark Helsop, who could nail three-pointers all night long. He and Call were true money players from the outside, and I knew they would make my game more effective underneath. The final person, although certainly not last of the potential starters, was Scott Moon. A WAC high jump champion, having jumped 7'2½", Scott was a real threat. He had served a mission in Pennsylvania, and I really looked up to him. Another returned missionary, Gary Trost, was also on the team, pushing me to be my very best. I'm sure, at 6'10", Gary would have loved to start. But I knew our year together would bode well for him to play center during the two years I was on a mission.

The Basketball Season Begins

After weeks of conditioning and practice, we began to jell and were finally ready to play ball! My classes were going quite well, and although the adjustment to college-level studies was pretty big, still I felt that I could handle it. As for playing, I was becoming more and more comfortable with the team and with their expectations of me. I knew that I would be learning and that I wouldn't have the same immediate impact that I had in high school, but that would be okay. My three-year stats at Emery High included averaging 20.3 points, 11.5 rebounds, and 5.4 blocked shots per game. In addition, our record during those years was 68-4. Major college ball was a quantum leap upward from high school, but I was confident that I could blend in and make a valid contribution.

Our first game, a warm-up against a Gent, Belgium team, was a good opportunity for us to get the kinks worked out. We won 94-77 and felt prepared psychologically to begin the Dodge NIT tournament the following night.

As we began our game against East Tennessee State, I was

feeling fantastic! The others fed me the ball, too, and I ended up with 23 points, 14 rebounds, and 5 blocked shots. I felt great, having played so well in our first official game of the season. That was the good news. The bad news was that they had been their conference champs the year before and returned all of their starting five. We hung in there, but the game ended 83-80 in their favor. It was a quick exit from the NIT, but we felt good about our performance.

The second game was the following Saturday, again in the Marriott Center. It was against in-state rival Utah State, and I scored 21 as we won 98-94. We knew that we'd be playing them again in just a week, with Weber State being our sole opponent until the rematch. We went to Ogden and were pleased with winning that game by 12 points, 69-57. Steve Schreiner scored 22 in that one, and we felt like we were on our way.

Our rematch in Logan was a totally different game from the week before, as they slowed the ball down considerably. We still won, though, by a five-point margin of 63-58, and it was during that contest that I came to appreciate the rabid Aggie fans! They were incredible, and we felt fortunate to have gotten out of there with a win.

For our next game, we flew east to Philadelphia, and played La Salle. Little did I know, as we touched down on Pennsylvania soil, that my professional career would begin there in just three short years. It wasn't a good omen for that game, however, as they beat us by 12, 93-81. It was a long flight back to Utah, and yet we were excited to be hosting the Cougar Classic in just two days, so we tried to shrug off the loss.

One of the great basketball traditions at the Y is the annual early December Cougar Classic, and I was excited to at last be part of it. Our first game was with Eastern Kentucky, and we had a high scoring contest, ending in a win. The final score was 90-86 in our favor, and I scored a personal high of 29 points. I was totally high during that game, almost unconscious, and I was happy that my folks had been able to be there and enjoy the victory with us. Because we lived so close, they had committed to attend all of our home games.

What I didn't anticipate was our loss the following night, against St. Johns. They beat us for the championship, 67-62, and that was a bitter pill for us to swallow. Nor did we fare any better the following Wednesday, when the Sun Devils from Arizona State came to Provo and beat us 82-74. I was high-point man for the third game in a row, with 22 points, but my focus was on team success, and I ached with this second loss in a row. It meant that our first eight games saw us with four wins against four losses. The losses were quite respectable, however, when we learned that the losses came against four teams that at that point in the season had a combined 23-3 record.

The Beginning of WAC Play

The rest of the preseason was the same roller coaster of winning and losing, but we felt like we were progressing, even though our record was six wins against seven losses. We didn't fare any better the first weekend of WAC competition, as we split on the western road trip. We won our first game against San Diego State, 73-61, but then arrived in Hawaii without a whole lot of energy. It was great being in the islands, though, and I tasted just enough of the tropical paradise to want to spend time there when I could just relax and enjoy myself. Hawaii beat us soundly, 74-65, and what made it even worse was the fact that Utah had beaten both of these teams, putting the Utes at the top after the first weekend of season play. Of course Utah was 13-1 at this point of the season, and with Josh Grant leading the way, they were the team we had to beat if we were going to end the season the way we wanted to.

We won our next two games in Provo, a doubleheader with UTEP and New Mexico. The win against New Mexico was particularly satisfying for me, since the press had been hyping the matchup between 7'2" Luc Longley and me. We were on opposite ends of our college career, and I had watched him play for what seemed like forever. It was a great contest, and I think both of us came out on the short end of things during the game. But we won, 72-65, and the score said it all for me. Actually, I couldn't wait to play against them in Albuquerque later in the season.

We then pounded Colorado State in Ft. Collins, 72-55, and we were all feeling better about things. I had 25 points in this last game, and it just served to motivate me against Wyoming, in Laramie, two days later. I tossed in 27 points in that game,

but we came out short, by an 86-80 score. That was the night I
found out what it's like to play basketball in Laramie, Wyoming.
I don't think I've ever seen more fanatical fans than those Cowboy folks. They were something else, and didn't let up for one
minute during that game. I think if I ever want to teach anyone
about fan support, I'll take them to Laramie and let them
watch a BYU-Wyoming game. It was awesome!

For me personally, college basketball was great fun, and I
felt like I was progressing to my expectations. I had been high-
point man in ten of our first fifteen games, and I felt good
about that. I share this statistic because it becomes relevant as
this season, and my story, progresses. Just as I was rolling along
at a record-setting pace, at least as far as blocked shots were
concerned, suddenly I felt like my whole world had dropped
out from beneath me, and I was groping in total darkness. It
began visibly with the Air Force game, which we won 72-55.
That was the good news. The bad news, for me, was that I hit
only two out of seven from the field, for a season low total of
seven points.

My Midseason Slump

Strange things happened to me during this time of year,
and looking back I think I understand why. From every direction I was getting advice about either going on a full-time mission or staying home to play ball. Most of that advice had good
merits for whichever position it supported. I was seriously
beginning to believe that I could serve a "mission" of sorts
regardless of what I chose. I reasoned that my whole life was a
mission. After all, as a member-representative of the Church—
both on and off the court—I could be an example for the Lord.
I was already very active in speaking at youth firesides and
other meetings.

After speaking with one of the General Authorities of the
Church, I concluded that I could serve the Lord whether I
served a full-time mission or served as a role model while playing ball. Playing ball and serving a mission at the same time—
how perfect! After all, other great professional LDS athletes
had made this choice, and they were successful and worthy of
following.

As I was wavering with my decision to serve the Lord full-time, I was starting to struggle with my grades, my love life, and my game. I began to see less and less playing time, until I was averaging five or six minutes on the floor per game. I just couldn't believe how rapidly my fortunes had changed. Life was becoming a very bitter pill to swallow each morning, and I was beginning to question even my very existence.

As far as WAC play was concerned, we won ten of our next thirteen games. But as for me, personally, I was totally erratic. The low moments were in scoring only four points against San Diego State, two points against New Mexico, two points against Air Force, and six points against Utah. I did score twenty points against Utah the other time we played them, but I was really tentative offensively. Thank goodness I was still rebounding and blocking shots, or I probably wouldn't have seen *any* playing time.

That was when a literal miracle occurred in my life. One day, while I was wallowing around in this mud of my own making, my bishop from Castle Dale, Scott Johansen, phoned. He said that he wanted to meet with me, and the sooner the better.

I naturally agreed to spend some time with him, and before I knew it, we were sitting across from each other and visiting.

"Shawn," he began quite firmly, "I've been sensing a need to visit with you for some time now. I appreciate your taking time from your busy schedule to see me."

Time? I questioned to myself. *What's so valuable about my time?* Instead of saying this, however, I simply shrugged and said, "Anytime, Bishop. You know I've always got time to see you."

"Let me get right to the point, then," he continued, taking a deep breath. "Shawn, your folks say that you're wavering about serving a mission. Is this true?"

"Well," I began, not knowing how to answer, "I . . . uh . . . I've been thinking that maybe basketball can be my mission . . . if you know what I mean, Bishop."

"I think I do, Shawn, and I can understand how you could reach this conclusion."

"Bishop," I interrupted, not wanting to be talked out of my decision, "I've even spoken with a General Authority about the difficulty of this decision. It somehow doesn't seem so cut and dried anymore."

"Perhaps," Bishop Johansen continued, "I could put it in a little different perspective . . . that is, if you would like me to."

"Sure, Bishop. Tell me anything that's on your mind."

"Well, Shawn, I was thinking about the other 47,000 missionaries who are out there serving. I suspect, if we were to have the ability to interview them, each one would have just as valid a reason, in their minds, why they shouldn't have taken time to accept a two-year call from the Lord—as do you. Oh, granted they aren't in the public eye like you are, but they do value their time. I'd bet each one of them could justify staying home from their mission, if they had a mind to. Whether it would be to run their father's farm, to become a physician, accept a scholarship to Harvard—there would be about 47,000 reasons.

"But you know what, Shawn?" he continued, smiling his All-American smile, "the Lord, through his prophet, has asked that *all* worthy young men serve a mission, not all but those who think they have a more important errand."

I really don't remember much else that was talked about that night, but I do remember the feeling I had in my heart as Bishop Johansen shared his feelings. I experienced one of the most profound impressions of my life, and I had no doubt as to what the Lord expected me to do. I was no better than any of my friends, I knew that; but I also knew through the whisperings of His Spirit to my spirit that I had to put Him first by serving a mission in His name. Even more important, as a life-long dream I had *wanted* to serve and to share with all my heart the message of the Savior's atonement and the restoration of His gospel. I had a burning sensation within me that is impossible to describe.

Long after Bishop Johansen left for his return trip to Castle Dale, I sat in quiet solitude. No longer did I have doubts about myself, my ability to pass my classes, or my priorities as a basketball player. I would take the spiritual gifts the Lord had blessed me with, especially my testimony of Jesus Christ, and I would trust that the Lord's servants would send me where these gifts could be fully utilized. Suddenly my shoulders seemed lighter, and my heart beat with an excitement I hadn't known in weeks. I would fill out my papers, take my physical and dental exams, and turn them into the bishop. Within weeks I would know where the Lord wanted me to serve! I was inwardly consoled, to say the least, and I was relieved that the cloud that had been following me had now dispersed and that sunny days were on the horizon. Now I couldn't wait to call Mom and Dad! They'd be ecstatic!

The WAC Tournament and Victory

As I expected, my folks *were* thrilled with my decision to go on a mission and were also relieved that the real Shawn was back among the living. And, as one would also suspect, I was able to again concentrate on schoolwork, so my grades came back up to where they needed to be. My exploits on the hard-court also improved, and I knew that if I applied myself, I could possibly even set an NCAA record for blocked shots. Maryland's Cedric Lewis and LSU's Shaquille O'Neal were both pushing my own pace, and I began to enjoy the pressure. Alonzo Mourning of Georgetown had set the pace with 169 blocks in a season, and reaching that summit seemed totally attainable.

But even more than my own stats, I wanted to measure up as a contributor to what was becoming a good basketball team. We were now approaching the WAC tournament in Laramie, and we hoped to play Utah for the championship. They had beaten us the last week of the regular season, 72-71, and we knew we were a better team than that.

Our first tournament game was against Colorado State, and we were totally ready to play. We hustled, and won by 13, 69-56. I scored 13 in that game and felt good about my all-around performance. I was also relieved that my family had safely arrived for the game, having traveled through some treacherous snow and ice storms from Utah.

This win set up a semifinal game against our nemesis, Hawaii. We had split with them during the regular season, and they had the capacity to beat us. The game was close right down to the wire, but we won 73-71. Utah also won their semi-final game, and so the championship was on the line. We would be assured an NCAA tournament bid with a win, but without it, we could very likely go to the National Invitational Tournament.

As we warmed up to play Utah, I felt the same adrenaline

rush I'd felt two years earlier as I was warming up to play Rich-field for Emery's first state championship. The difference now, though, was that the University of Utah basketball program was ranked eighth in the nation in the AP and UPI polls, and the stakes were huge! I'll have to hand it to Coach Majerus of Utah: he came out onto the floor during warm-ups wearing a Wyoming sweater. The crowd went wild, and we knew Utah had just gained the home crowd advantage. On a personal note, Mom was pretty ill and so had opted to stay in the motel and watch the game on TV. I felt bad that she wasn't in attendance and that she wasn't feeling well; I just hoped that I played well for her and that we would be smiling a couple of hours from then.

The game finally got underway, and as we expected, it see-sawed back and forth for the entire forty minutes. Finally, with 1:27 left in regulation, the score was knotted 42-42. Nathan Call drove and scored with fifteen seconds remaining, and was fouled in the process. We were now ahead 44-42, and he was at the line. But he missed his foul shot, and Utah came down the floor with a vengeance. They got the ball to Walter Watts, whom I was guarding, with four seconds left. He scored, and I fouled him on his shot. That meant that he could give their team a victory by hitting his foul shot. I was upset at myself for committing the foul, and I just hoped he would miss so we could go into overtime.

Watts did miss, and before we could get the ball down the court, time expired, taking us into the overtime I had hoped for. When play resumed, I was able to get the tip to Call, but we weren't able to score. Neither was Utah, though, as we went up and down without getting an advantage.

Finally, with three minutes remaining in overtime, Trost was fouled. He made one of the shots, and we were ahead 45-44. Byron Wilson of Utah was then fouled, and he likewise made one of his two shots. So, we were again tied up 45 all with 2:30 left to play. Then, with 1:50 to play, Trost was again fouled. This time, however, he made both of his free throws, and we had a 47-45 advantage. To cinch it for us, with forty-five seconds remaining, Moon drove through the middle and scored a lay-up, putting us up 49-45. We felt pretty good going back down the court, but then, with thirty seconds remaining, Byron Wilson connected on a three-point shot and was fouled in the process of shooting. He made his foul shot, and we were stunned to think they had made up the four-point deficit.

With the score tied at 49 all, and with eight seconds remaining, Call was again fouled. I'll have to give him credit because he was one cool customer as he stepped to the line. He made both of his free throws, and we were sure of the victory. That was when something confusing happened, as I was taken out of the game. I couldn't understand Coach's decision, especially since we had to intimidate their shot. But I had long before determined to let my coaches do the coaching, and so I concentrated on what was happening on the floor.

At that second, a fluke happened, and Utah found Tyrone Tate all alone under the basket, with no one defending him. They passed him the ball, and he went up for an unmolested lay-up—and missed! But no one was around him yet, so he got his own rebound and put it up a second time. He was under the basket, alone, but the second shot also rimmed out, and the final buzzer sounded with our winning 51-49. We were the WAC tournament champions, and I think I must have jumped a mile high in celebration!

When the noise finally subsided, and we had cut down the net, the awards were presented. I was honored to have been named to the all-tournament team and to be the tournament MVP. My dad just beamed, and I'll have to admit this was one of the greatest thrills of my life. It was a dream come true, and the crowd that had been partisan to Utah sat stunned, not believing that we had dethroned the eighth-ranked team in the country. The win was a total team and coaching effort, and the few Y fans in attendance let us know how excited they were with our win.

That night, instead of bussing to Colorado and then flying home with the team, Coach Reid allowed me to return to Utah with my family. So we stayed at a small motel in Laramie. The city was so packed that it was hard to find a room. The next morning I wanted to thank the motel owner for accommodating my folks, so I signed a ball and gave it to him. They seemed pretty happy with the gift, and we were happy to have a way to show our appreciation to them.

We made it home okay, and then met with the entire team and coaching staff on KSL TV's *Sports Beat Sunday*, with Craig Bollerjack. Following that, we all went home and crashed, knowing the following week would be hectic as we prepared for the NCAA tournament. We found out that day that we had been assigned to the first round of the Western Regionals, in Salt Lake City, so we were pretty happy about that—no road travel and more time to concentrate on our studies and to prepare for our first-round opponent, Virginia, from the Atlantic Coast Conference.

Before we knew it, Thursday arrived, and we found ourselves in the Huntsman Center warming up for our game. The game was to be nationally televised, and so we wanted to present the Y and the WAC in the best image possible. They had beat the Y a decade earlier, in the Ralph Sampson days, and we wanted to make restitution for that loss.

It was a great game, too, and we won quite handily, 61-48. For the time I played, I was able to score 8 points and pull down 5 rebounds. The best part of my game, though, was defense, where I set an NCAA tournament record by blocking 10 shots. I had a great time intimidating the Volunteers, and I felt good that we had shown the country that we were capable of winning on that level.

Two days later we were matched up against powerhouse Arizona, from Tucson. Coach Lute Olsen had developed a great team, and we were excited to play them. We played well, too, and even had the lead at one point in the second half. But then they got ahead, I fouled out, and we never could get the lead back. They finally won by 12 points, sending us home for the season.

I felt badly that we had exited the tournament in the second round, but I also felt proud that our team had progressed so far from where we were at the first of the year. We had been picked to finish fifth in the conference, and yet we had proven that we could play with the best teams in the country and hold our own. It was truly a season to remember.

Receiving My Mission Call

Three weeks after putting my mission papers in, the call arrived at the post office in Castle Dale. I was in Provo, so Dad called me, and said, "Shawn, I've got something sitting here for you." I'd called him every day during that week to see if the call had arrived, so I knew what he was talking about. I grabbed my friends, Rebecca and Amy Kimmel, hopped in my '72 GMC pickup, and nearly flew home.

When I arrived, Dad was home alone, with the envelope unopened. The rest of the family was gone. Mom and my sisters were in Salt Lake City, shopping, and I knew they'd kill me if I opened it without them. Finally, when they didn't return, Justin came home on our Honda motorcycle, and I was so nervous that I went for a ride, just so I wouldn't be around that envelope.

By this time it was about five o'clock in the afternoon, and I still couldn't go into the house because of my call. Dad could tell what I was going through, so he came out and indicated that they'd understand if I went ahead and opened it. I agreed, so I went in and the rest of us sat around as I opened the envelope. When I read the words from the prophet, Ezra Taft Benson, telling me that I had been assigned to the Australia Sydney Mission, I jumped off the chair I was sitting on, gave everyone a big hug, and was ecstatic! About an hour later, Mom and my sisters came home to the news. Mom started crying, she was so happy, and the rest of the evening I just drove around showing my call to my friends and relatives.

Finishing School

Taking finals, once again, was horrendous! Just like the end of the first semester, I had a knot in my gut that didn't go away until I walked out of the testing center having completed my last exam. I didn't know if college life got easier as time passed, but I surely know the relief and sheer joy of making it through another semester.

Bidding my friends good-bye was even tougher than I thought it would be, but I managed my final farewells and loaded up the GMC for the return trip to Castle Dale. I knew I wouldn't see most of them until after my mission, and the thoughts of being away for two years became heavier with each passing day. Still, I knew I would have a couple of weeks to relax and enjoy myself at home, so the full impact of my mission had not settled in.

Returning home was great, and in between trips back to
Provo to purchase my mission clothes, I made a stab at helping
around the house. Dad and Mom had started fixing up Adrianne's room. While Dad painted the trim in her room, I came
in, and we had a great one-on-one chat. I said something to him
that I hope he always remembers and that should have totally
boosted his ego. I told him that when I dated girls at the Y, several of them had complimented me on my manners and how
well I treated them. They told me more than once that Dad
must have treated Mom pretty special for me to have learned
how to treat them. I passed the compliment on to Dad, and he
smiled a mile wide. I then thanked him for treating Mom with
the courtesy he extended and for setting that example for me.
In all, it was one of the best talks we've had and sort of set the
tone for our relationship in the days that followed.

14 May was a hallmark day for me in that I accompanied
my folks and many of our family on a trip to the Manti
Temple. While I will explain the purpose of temples in the last
chapter of the book, let me just mention that this was a day I
had looked forward to for years. It was a day when I entered
the House of the Lord and there made promises to Him that
are too sacred to share. I knew that I would be walking along a
higher path from this day forth, and this was somewhat fright-
ening. I thought of what the Savior said on the Sermon on the
Mount, about "where much is given, much is required," and I
knew that the Lord would require a more exacting lifestyle
from me than ever before. That evening, as we made our way
back through the mountain passes to Castle Dale, I felt a
sense of peace and understanding that far surpassed my expectations.

Two days later, Mom and I went to Provo, and I had an
experience that was as painful as our trip to the temple had
been pleasant. During the basketball season, I had broken my
nose while playing a game. It had become increasingly difficult
for me to breathe, so I went into surgery, and had my nose
reset. I don't actually remember much about the surgery, other
than what the nurses told me afterward. They said that I was
totally obnoxious and that I harassed them to no end. I don't
remember it, though, and so in my mind it never happened. I
do remember the pain afterwards, however, and Mom and I

stayed in Provo for the night so I could have the nasal packing removed the next day.

By the time we got back to Castle Dale, Dad was busy with the Kimmel family, setting forms to pour cement for a deck on the north side of the house. They borrowed a cement mixer to make the job easier, and I guess it worked because before long the job was done and they were sitting around eating. As for me, I was pretty much out of it with sedatives, and I just lay around sipping 7Up.

My Farewell

Almost before I knew it, 26 May had arrived, and with it came what seemed like endless cars of people to attend my mission farewell at our church. The meeting was awesome, as in addition to Mom, Dad, Justin, Adrianne, and me speaking, my Aunt Jo Jo sang and played the harp, and then accompanied my sister, Tasha, as she sang her first solo in public. The impact of seeing a stake-conference-size group of friends and relatives there to show their love and support of my mission was absolutely incredible.

Afterward, my folks outdid themselves in feeding a hot roast beef dinner to about two hundred friends and family members. Dad had spent four hours the day before cutting the lawns, and everything looked fantastic, with the best weather of spring. Aunt Jo Jo also set her harp up in the strawberry patch and played to everyone's content. She really added a touch of class to our day.

Being Set Apart as a Missionary

Without a doubt the most significant moment of preparation for my mission came the following Tuesday night. President Arnold, our stake president, invited us to join him for a meeting to set me apart *from* the world and *for* my missionary labors. I was flooded with feelings as he and others holding the Melchizedek Priesthood placed their hands on my head and set me apart as a missionary for The Church of Jesus Christ of

Latter-day Saints. During that blessing, they granted to me the power, rights, and responsibilities of an embassador of the Lord, and then added a special blessing of health and strength to sustain me throughout.

When President Arnold concluded the blessing, I knew in my heart that it hadn't been his blessing but that he was only the mouthpiece, as it had come directly from the Lord. I knew that I was now a commissioned servant of the Savior, and the feeling of responsibility and excitement gave me a new understanding of the word *joy*. As the scripture states, I was filled with a peace that "passeth all understanding" (Philippians 4:7).

I knew that as of that hour, I would never be the same Shawn Bradley. I was now referred to as *Elder*, a title that was worth more than all of the national championships in the world. Somehow the word *basketball* seemed insignificant at this moment, and I realized more than ever before that athletics should be kept in perspective and could be used as an effective tool. On the other hand, those who allowed sports to become an all-encompassing religion on its own had no idea what life—and the atonement of Jesus Christ—was all about.

These were some of my thoughts as I knelt at my bedside that night, knowing that although I wouldn't see my bed, or my family, for the next twenty-four months, I would serve as did the Apostle Paul of old. I would have a song in my heart and a skip in my step, and my steps would be measured as I went into homes to teach the restored truths of the Savior's gospel. I was really *wired*, to put it mildly. But I was also at peace with myself, as I knew my decision to leave my future with basketball in the Lord's hands to do with as He saw fit somehow seemed like the perfect thing to do.

6

Two Years Down Under

The Missionary Training Center

Arriving at the Missionary Training Center, or MTC, just a few blocks from where I had played ball in the Marriott Center, was an awesome feeling. It was weird being in Provo and not having my truck there to chase around and see my buds or to go on dates. Of course, dates were out of my mind for the next two years, and even though I knew it would be an adjustment, I was actually looking forward to concentrating on my relationship with the Lord rather than with girls. I loved the thought of what the next weeks would bring as I learned the ropes of missionary service.

My family joined me for an orientation meeting, and then before we knew what was happening, I was invited to say good-bye and leave through one door, while they were asked to leave through another. Only those who have shared that experience know how gut wrenching it is to bid farewell, then watch one's family walk down the hallway and out of sight. It was no different for us, as I hugged my sisters and brother, then Mom and Dad. They were the greatest support system a guy could have, and I couldn't remember feeling more love for them than I felt at that moment.

But soon they were gone, and I found myself in a sea of

2,500 white shirts. It was so great being a part of the Lord's army, and as I learned my new companion's name, Elder Kenneth Roberts, I couldn't believe my ears. He was the very same Ken Roberts who was my roommate in college, and my teammate on the basketball squad. With this strange coincidence, I knew that somehow my life would never be the same. Ken was on his way to Australia as well, but he was off to the Melbourne mission, and the supervisors at the MTC had decided to allow us to spend our time there as roommates. The exciting thing for us was that they had brought our eight-foot beds over from John Hall and installed them in our room. So when we first walked in, we were blown away to see our already-broken-in beds waiting for us, linen and all. Were we ever relieved!

While I'll not detail the next two plus weeks of my life, I will say that never have I had such a capsulized growth experience! We were blessed to sit at the feet of the Apostles and other General Authorities and to learn what being a servant of the Lord is all about.

In some ways, I didn't want my MTC experience to end, but I also couldn't wait to fly out of the United States and begin my missionary life in Australia.

That day arrived almost before I could believe it, and soon I was at the airport with my family, saying a *final* good-bye. This farewell wasn't as emotional, though, as the anticipation of what the Lord had in store for me over the next two years was so all-consuming and exciting.

We laughed and had a great couple of hours together, and then after taking some pictures, I waved good-bye and ducked into the plane. As we taxied down the runway and then lifted off and headed west out over the Salt Lake Valley, I couldn't help but think of what that valley must have looked like 150 years earlier as Brigham Young and the early Saints came down through the canyon and gazed upon the barren wasteland. They had truly made it blossom like a rose in the desert, and now it was my turn to go out and proclaim the same truths that they gave literally every comfort of life to support—including their lives. My great-grandparents had likewise crossed the plains with that same conviction, and somehow I felt like an honored part of this great heritage, being blessed with the opportunity of teaching concepts that gave the greatest joy.

Arriving in Sydney and My First Area

After twenty hours of travel, we touched down in Australia and were greeted by President and Sister Brent Nash, as well as the mission home staff. Following a quick orientation, I collapsed in bed for a while and then prepared fo receive my first assignment. I was surprised to learn that I would be staying right there in Sydney, working with a companion that was part of the mission staff, but this allowed me to sleep on the floor with a special 4 1/2' by 8' mattress that had been purchased for me.

When I was finally transferred, I was given permission to simply roll up my mattress and take it with me to my next area. This practice became routine for me, so I slept almost every night of my mission on that mattress.

The other convenience I enjoyed was the use of an automobile. I rode a bike for just two weeks and was in a walking area for about two and a half months; other than that, I was able to drive a Church-owned car. I don't know whether my leaders were afraid I might get hit by a train or something if I rode a bike, or whether they were just trying to protect my knees and joints for a future on the hardcourt. Actually, neither of these reasons may have been valid, since my proselyting area was the size of the state of Utah, and we had to work with other missionaries in addition to our own contacts. In looking back, it was probably simply impractical for me to have done my work without a car.

Knocking on Doors

One of the most difficult yet humbling activities we engaged in was what we call tracting, or knocking on the doors of people who aren't expecting us. We would begin this experience in prayer and invite the Lord to direct us to those Aussie people who were interested in learning more about the Savior and His gospel. We didn't want to be offensive to anyone, but at the same time, we wanted to tell the entire world what made us such a unique and happy people.

I wish I could say that most Aussies were interested in our

message, but truthfully they weren't. They were usually gracious to us, and were *always* stunned for a moment when they saw me looking down on them. But in the main, they were content with the religion they already had. I learned to use my size to my advantage, though, and would tell folks about who I was, explain my basketball career that I'd put on hold, and share how excited I was to be with my companion sharing a message of such eternal consequence.

Working with Polynesians

One of the great blessings of my mission was in working with the humble, Christlike people from the Polynesian islands. One of these families, the Torgis, was especially good to us. We were able to teach their cousins, Ross and Brenda Tarawa, and baptize them and three of their daughters. Actually, the three daughters were baptized on one day, and later I baptized Ross. Afterward, we ordained him to the office of priest in the Aaronic Priesthood. This allowed him to re-enter the waters of baptism, this time taking his wife and baptizing her.

I loved that family so much, and the girls were just like little sisters to me. I wrote and told my folks, "What a wonderful race of people the Polynesians are—especially when they have the gospel and live it in their lives." That was how I felt, too, and I will always love the Torgis and the Tarawas.

Support from Home

Like every other missionary in the world, one of the greatest moments of a mission is in hearing from family and friends at home. For me it was no different, and even though I didn't park next to the mailbox waiting for a letter, when one came it lifted my spirits and gave me strength.

I especially enjoyed hearing from my family, and in a letter dated 2 September 1991, Dad said the following:

Shawn, I'm so proud of you and what you are doing, and am really glad to hear all the neat things that are happening to you. I know it is not all easy, nor peaches and roses around every corner—but take strength in knowing that our prayers and support are always with you.

Dad then shared personal items of interest from home and concluded with these words:

> Well, my son, time to go. Stand as strong in the Gospel as you stand strong in the world! We just love hearing about your progress and experiences.
>
> I love you, Dad

A month after writing the above letter, Dad wrote the most profound letter of my mission. In it, he shared his own conversion experience while living in Germany right after my birth. Although he had shared it with me before in person, reading such a faith-promoting account—and knowing it was my father who had experienced it for my ultimate benefit—was especially profound.

I loved hearing from Mom, too, and from my other family members. I couldn't believe the photos I received and how grown-up my brother and sisters had become. In response to one of these letters, I wrote back to my sister Tasha with the following:

"Hey, my most beautiful younger sister, who is in college turning every head of all those guys who want a beautiful wife! I think you can have some competition, however. I just received a letter from Mom, and a picture of Adrianne. She looked 17! I don't know why I got stuck in such a 'good looking' family. I guess there has to be an ugly duckling in every lot." I drew a smiley face at this point in the letter, and then continued to ask Tasha about her life at college.

With supportive letters like these coming and going regularly, there was no way for me to fail. I knew of the power of prayer, and I also knew of the volume of prayers being offered in my behalf by those who were continuing their lives at home. It was just great to receive love from home while serving the ultimate errand of love in the name of the Savior.

Media Exposure

One of the exciting yet sometimes burdensome aspects of my mission was the constant requests for me to share my missionary activities with news media, especially the Aussie television stations. Our missionaries thought this was great, since it gave my companions and me the opportunity to explain our purpose in the country and to testify of the Savior. They also took plenty of video footage of our knocking on doors, and I was happy they did since it became an icebreaker for later conversations.

In one interview, a reporter asked me if I would accept a financial offer to turn pro during the two-year period of my mission. I told them I was in Australia for another purpose, that missionary work was now paramount in my life, and that basketball would always be there. That's honestly how I felt, too, because a mission was a sacred time to devote solely to building the kingdom of God, while basketball was simply a game to enjoy, another form of entertainment. When I contrasted bringing people to a knowledge of the Savior to bringing them a couple of hours of excitement through basketball the question seemed shallow and a bit absurd.

One of the most meaningful interviews I had was at the temple site in Sydney. It was with a host of the show called *A Current Affair*. I was especially excited for the Church to have this exposure, since the show was so popular that between three and five million viewers tuned in. The feedback we received was so positive, and hopefully it opened many avenues for the missionary program.

Mission Growth

To illustrate how quickly the Church grew within my mission boundaries, by the end of my first year, when I had been in the country for about six months, our 200 missionaries had assisted about 170 people into the Church. My last year, even after our mission had split and there were only about 150 of us serving, we witnessed over 700 people embrace the gospel. It was thrilling to be a part of that phenomenal growth, but it was even more exciting to work with one individual, or one family, and see their lives change as they walked down into the waters of baptism.

The Fruits of Labor

One of the great opportunities of working with President Keith Nielsen, who replaced President Nash in July 1991, was to attend our regularly scheduled zone conferences. Our mission has several zones, or groups of missionaries, and meeting with them was always a spiritual feast. On one such occasion, I was especially excited to attend a conference in one of my former areas, called Canberra. Not only was I looking forward to meeting with a lot of my fellow missionaries, but a young man I had baptized while serving there was now going to be interviewed by President Nielsen to determine his worthiness to receive the Melchizedek Priesthood. His name was Brent Miller, and almost a year earlier, when my companion and I were teaching him the gospel, I felt of his great potential. He had that something extra in his makeup that would make him a great addition to the Church in Canberra. So he had been baptized, had grown in the Aaronic Priesthood, and was now ready to be ordained an elder in the Melchizedek Priesthood.

President Nielsen met with him, determined his worthiness and his increased understanding of the priesthood, and recommended his ordination. When President Nielsen told me of his experience with Brent, I couldn't wait to share my excitement with my family back home. In writing to them, I repeated what I have shared here, and then concluded with the following statement:

"President Nielsen came out of the room after completing his interview with [Brent Miller], and told me that this baptism made my whole mission. It is so great to be a part of this great work the Lord has prepared. I know that we are His children, and we're helping others to be able to take part in the same promised blessings we now enjoy. The people, or 'sheep,' we find have the same promises and rights we do, if they accept the message of the restoration."

These were my feelings as I thought of Brent, and of the

others I had seen enter the waters of baptism. His life had made a full 180-degree turn since his conversion, and I couldn't be more happy for him—and for the blessing the gospel will be to him and his family.

An Interesting Diversion

I can't quite say when it all began, but somewhere later in my mission, I would occasionally get some inner feelings telling me how right it would be to play professional basketball sooner than anyone might have imagined. If I allowed my mind to toy with these images for very long, they would begin to affect the work I was doing. I realized that these thoughts could become all-consuming, and so I learned a great lesson from this simple conflict. If I was going to do missionary work, I'd better put my whole heart into it, because anything else I considered would begin to immediately detract from the work at hand.

As my mission progressed, these thoughts would naturally play across the stage of my mind. On one of these occasions, I went to my mission president, whom I had grown very close to. He had become a father to me, but more than that, he could counsel, advise, and enlighten me on any problem that might arise. After presenting my feelings to him, I found it amazing that he had experienced similar feelings about my going directly into the pros at the conclusion of my mission. Even so, he suggested that before I entertain these feelings further, I first determine whether the NBA would even consider me.

As a result of this conversation, we enlisted some close friends who were very knowledgeable about the workings of the NBA. They reported back that I was, in fact, projected as one of the top picks, even at this early stage of my collegiate career. This information further distracted from my missionary work, and President Nielsen suggested that I make a decision "one way or the other, and then stick to this decision," so I could get back to the missionary task at hand.

Somewhere in the middle of this activity, and unbeknownst to me, Dad and his cousin, Laury Hammel, were initiating an investigation of their own. Laury is a tennis pro, and because of his connections, he had opportunity to speak with several professional agents. The topic of my future would come up, and one thing leading to another resulted in my dad and Laury meeting with five of the top NBA agents in February, during the NBA all-star weekend in Salt Lake City. At the time, Dad thought he was just getting a head start in learning about the NBA so he could help me in making decisions down the road.

During that exciting weekend, Dad and Laury followed through with their plans, holding private interviews with five of the industry's top agents. While Dad was asking these men pre-planned questions, he had his tape recorder going, recording every word they said. He was especially surprised to learn their consensus opinion that if I opted for the draft without returning to the Y, I would likely be a top-five choice. He then charted out these conversations, listing the agents by order with their answers and then writing down his impressions of each of them—truly an abridgment of a very long and exhausting weekend.

I was therefore surprised when one day I received a large envelope from home and found this agent chart enclosed. While I didn't want anything to distract from my missionary labors, still I couldn't get out of my mind the gnawing feeling that was increasing inside of me. One morning, after fervent prayer, I knew as well as I had known anything in my life that I was supposed to forfeit my last three years of playing at the Y and enter the NBA in the last of June at the time of the draft.

This final decision was mine, and mine alone. I had been reared to make my own decisions; something this important would be something the Lord and I had to work out. Nevertheless, I sought guidance from my mission president and from my companion, simply because so much was at stake in this decision. I had also come to learn that in receiving direction from the Lord, if the feelings were strong and constant, they were valid. But if they waxed and waned and were all over the wall, I could pretty much lay claim as being the source of them. I also know, however, that the Lord expected me to do my homework; so I was especially grateful for the effort my dad had expended in my behalf.

So many things went through my mind in considering this momentous decision that I can't even begin to describe them all. But these thoughts included my former teammates, close

friends, avid BYU fans, family, and what they all would think
about my not returning to play ball for the Y. Dating, finding
an eternal companion, and the joys of college social life were
also in there somewhere.

During this time, my mission president asked me what I *felt*
I should do, and I gave him a straightforward response. He
then directed me to immediately call my parents and inform
them. Was I ever nervous! I had no idea how they would really
take this news. I found out later that they had no idea how I
would take it, but that they had come to the same conclusion
without sharing their impressions with me. Their concern, of
course, was whether they should call me in Australia and dis-
turb my work by sharing their feelings with me.

I made the call on 1 April, totally surprising them. After
telling them of my decision to turn pro, the feeling of peace
and joy was indescribable. I knew what I needed to do, they
knew what I needed to do, and in that wonderful moment, two
realms half a world apart meshed into one. The love and support I received from my mom and dad just reinforced the answer
I had received on my knees.

I knew the flack I would take from a lot of folks who were
counting on me to fulfill my previous commitment to the Y, but
I also knew that if I didn't follow the impressions I had received,
the Church and principle of receiving answers to prayer would
be for me null and void. I really believed the words from Shake-
speare's *Hamlet*: "This above all, to thine own self be true; and
it must follow, as the night the day, thou canst not then be false
to any man."

I knew there would be disappointment and anger over my
decision, but I had no idea the hue and cry that would spread
across the land. Angry letters to the editor appeared in the
Provo and Salt Lake City newspapers, and hate mail came to
me through my parents' mailbox. In addition, numerous phone
calls were placed, deriding my judgment and decision, basically
saying that I had no character since I was going back on my
commitment to play for the Y at least one more year. Not one
of these responses failed to mention that they were avid
Cougar fans.

Although my intent in sharing this experience isn't to
appear defensive or to share the negative, let me just share the

gist of one letter from Logan. In it, the man said: "May the IRS have its way with you. You have your money and no one has your apologies." While I have to admit that I had considered the fact that a future salary cap on entering NBA players had been considered, my decision had to do with much, much more, and really comes back to the inner peace I felt after inquiring of the Lord and then talking with my parents. Oh, I won't represent that I hadn't thought of the money, but I am a guy who grew up ranching with my Grandpa without any thought of wages. I just figured it was part of my obligation as a family member. In addition, I was someone who had worked for $4.55 an hour at Tracy's Texaco and who was being financially supported by my family during the past two years. Money was simply not a focus in my life. I honestly couldn't see what a person could do with more than a million dollars, anyway, other than to make their life easier, pay more taxes and tithing, and then help those who were needy and deserving. Those were good thoughts, and I certainly entertained them, but the money incentive just wasn't there for me when making my decision to turn pro.

In the midst of the aftermath of my announcement, I was happy to receive a letter from my dad, wherein he included Coach Roger Reid's reaction. Coach Reid said, "We are devastated to lose such a great player. We were counting on having [Shawn] another year after his mission. This leaves us in somewhat of a bind to replace him. It's tough to replace a player of that magnitude. We wish him every bit of success, and we have appreciated what he has done for our basketball program, and me personally. We wish him great success in the NBA. There is one sad coach in the WAC, and nine happy ones."

I could really understand Coach Reid's feelings of frustration and anxiety with my ill-timed announcement and how unsettling my decision would be to the Cougars' team make-up. I knew it wasn't easy for him to make this statement, so Coach Reid's dignity in wishing me success was even that much more appreciated.

In an extension of this statement, let me reiterate that I truly consider myself a Cougar and will always be proud to state that I am an alumnus of such an outstanding school and basketball program. I can't imagine a school of greater moral fiber. I had found it to be an institution of higher learning that emphasizes building character—the molding of the "total person." My experience with the athletic department, the professors, and the other students will always stand out as some of the finest hours of my life. I'll certainly be the Coug's greatest fan as this coming season begins!

For the time being, though, let me return to the difficult days following my announcement to turn pro. At that time, my mom was quoted in the Salt Lake *Tribune* as saying: "The reaction put our family's life into a spin. We had no idea we would get hate mail." In addition to the mail that went to Castle Dale, I received several letters from around the world, letting me know how off base I was. Four missionaries in Europe even wrote, seriously questioning my decision and my level of spirituality. When Dad was interviewed, he supported me by saying, "Shawn had enough resolve about his decision that these responses bothered him, but he didn't waver in the least with what he felt he had to do." When I was asked if I felt comfortable with my decision, I responded with, "Absolutely. Even when I first made the decision, I was sure. Everything that's happened in my life since then has just reassured it."

Perhaps this would be a good place to share a thought. A friend of mine once told me what Elder Henry Eyring of our Church General Authorities shared with him. Elder Eyring said, "When the elephants come to town, all the dogs bark." I knew that in many ways I was an elephant, someone larger than life. I also knew that I had come to Provo and that I needed to walk gently and cautiously so as not to step on any toes and offend anyone. But I have found that elephants do attract attention and that there are those who innocently and with good intent bark and allow unpleasant things to come out of their mouths—even when they haven't walked a mile in another's moccasins. In this case they are my gym shoes, rather than moccasins. I truly don't condemn these people for expressing their feelings, but I do feel badly that folks placed claim on my agency to do what I felt was best for me to do.

In another way, these people were totally justified in expressing their opinions. I had made that commitment out of the innocence of my seventeen-year-old youth and the pressure that was placed upon me to please people and say what they wanted me to say. From where I then stood, it was the perfectly logical thing to forecast. But if I had learned anything while tromping the streets of Australia, it was that I had two people to answer to in this life (at least until I got married), and they were my Heavenly Father and myself. To have selfishly acted against the impressions I received, would have been tantamount to denouncing my testimony of the truthfulness of the gospel. I knew the Church of Jesus Christ truly had been restored to the earth, and I knew that personal revelation was one of the great blessings of having the gift of the Holy Ghost. And so, in the face of criticism and rebuke, I quietly asked Heavenly Father to soften the hearts of those who didn't know the full story, and to give me the strength to pursue the course that I knew had been shown me. Once this had taken place, I was able to put the matter behind me, and continue my missionary labors.

I can't close this page of my life without sharing the fact that in addition to the negative letters about my turning pro, my family and I also received many, many more letters and phone calls offering support of my decision. While it would be self-serving to share all of these comments at this time, I would like to mention just three. The first came in the form of a letter, the second as a phone call to my folks, and the third in an interview for the *Daily Universe*, BYU's student newspaper.

Brother George Durrant, who had been president of the Missionary Training Center when I entered my mission and who was now a professor at the Y, wrote and said this: "I love you, my big friend, and I always will. I look forward to following your career with great joy and delight. May the Lord bless you as you return home and take on the tremendous challenges which lie ahead, challenges which you are very much up to. You and the Lord will be able to do it, and I know you found out long ago that in partnership with Him, all things are possible."

Brother Durrant's words pretty much summed up the comments of most of those who wrote, and I was humbled with the faith and confidence he and they had in my decision.

Of the many phone calls my folks received, the one that I appreciated more than I can say was from Coach Charles Bradley, one of the assistant basketball coaches from the Y. He had played successfully in the pros, as I previously mentioned, and he had even used David Falk—whom I was considering— as his agent. Anyway, he called and gave his complete and total support for my decision to turn pro. He said that if a person looked intelligently at my options, they would see that I could have made no other choice. That was a class phone call, and I will always appreciate him for making it. Finally, the newspaper interview. I was unaware of it at the time, of course, but someone sent it to my folks, and they passed it along to me. It was an interview with Utah's coach, Rick Majerus. For someone who does not share my religious beliefs, he said some pretty powerful things. When asked if he could empathize with Coach Reid, he gave a rather lengthy response that I would like to share. Among other things, he said the following:

> I think there is no question that Bradley has shown a commitment to the highest of values over and above his own academic endeavors. He has done this with belief in his God and his faith. I'm a big fan of Bradley.
>
> When my guys go on missions, I tell them to go on a mission—that is a higher calling. I don't believe in it— I'm not going to lie to you. But I believe in them and I have a lot of respect and admiration for them.
>
> I know Bradley doesn't do anything with a basketball on his mission. I understand those missions. I understand the tediousness of it. And I respect them for their beliefs, the kind of people they are, what the mission does and the fact that you lead a contemplative life of your own and you get in touch with God in your own way.
>
> I myself don't know if there is a God, or not. I've kind of fought that battle my whole life. If you've made that quantum leap of faith, you nurture it and you believe in it. I think there are a lot of benefits to that. I envy them in some ways.
>
> I tell you what I resent and what upsets me. Everyone is down on Bradley like he has been disloyal. He hasn't been disloyal to anybody. First of all, he's shown the ultimate loyalty to his religion and to his God. Above God, who do you want to be loyal to? That escapes me.

There is no question that this is the best decision. As I said, I really feel [his leaving] hurts Utah, too. It hurts the exposure of the league, the scheduling, the notoriety of the league. If we beat Bradley, it's a big thing for us.

I recruited the last two years with the idea that we were going to play Shawn Bradley. I got some guys who came in, liking that idea. They were naive guys in thinking they would be able to beat him.

I'll tell you what, I harbor no animosity or ill will toward BYU. I don't engage in that. [BYU has] a very good team. They are just losing the best player in America. [Shawn] is going to have an outstanding future. He is a great player.

I want to mention that Coach Rick Majerus from the University of Utah has been a close friend ever since high school. And even though I opted to play for the Y, he has still shown a great deal of class by supporting me through the years. I've always had respect for his coaching skills and for his knowledge of the game—and for his genuine love affair with life. With this article, I gained an appreciation for how willing he is to speak out in support of someone, giving them the assistance they need, regardless of how unpopular that assistance may be.

At this time, however, I'll let Coach Majerus's statements, as well as the others, stand on their own. Suffice it to say, I was more than a little thankful for the words that were spoken in my behalf and for the trust these friends showed in me and in my decision to move forward in my life as I knew I must.

My Final Weeks as a Full-time Missionary

Now that the announcement was out, my mind was again filled with peace. Because of NBA deadlines, I couldn't have waited to make this announcement after I had completed my mission. So, I did what I had to do and could now set my future plans aside to concentrate on finishing what the Lord had sent me out to do.

I was consumed with the need to finish my mission in a

sprint, knowing that those missionaries who slacked off were usually those who were also unable to finish other phases of their lives. I wanted to be able to look myself in the mirror with the knowledge that I had given the Lord a full measure with my mission assignment, and I knew this was the only way I could leave.

In fact, if the full truth were known, I really wasn't sure I wanted my mission to end. To date, it had by far been the most growth-producing and fulfilling experience of my life, and I had learned to love the Aussie people as though they were my own. I had spent two years laughing with them, crying with them, teaching them, and serving them; and the profound exhilaration I received was not something I wanted to lose.

And so, even though I knew I must use my mission as a launching pad for my life's pursuits, and savor each day, I worked to my fullest so that I could accomplish what I had been sent out to do.

My Final Six Weeks

After serving as an assistant to President Nielsen for several months, I had the great blessing of being released from that leadership position and spending my final month and a half knocking on doors—working directly with the people in a town called Campbelltown. My companion was Elder McGoon from Fiji, and we had many great experiences together. These weeks were some of the most fulfilling of my mission. I hardly thought about home and my future in the NBA; rather, I was consumed with the work, almost frightened that I would be released before I had finished the task I'd been sent across the ocean to complete.

With a week left in the country, my problems with the press increased. CNN came down for an interview, and ESPN was calling, not to mention the others. But I vowed that I would work until I climbed on the plane, and I intended to keep focused on the missionary work at hand. So, rather than get involved with the press, I simply said no to all requests for an interview. They were obviously upset, but I hadn't inquired of them; rather, I told them that when I arrived back in the states, I would respond to an interview.

In addition to this pressure, there was the problem I was having as I faced a change of lifestyle, with my full-time proselyting efforts coming to a close. Finally, with just a couple of days left on my mission, my emotions just got the best of me. I simply started to cry. I was lying on my specially made eight-foot bed, curled up in a fetal position and staring at a vaulted ceiling two inches from my forehead. I was still wearing my suit, which by now had seen more hours of wear than a suit ought to endure, and yet my mind was confused, not wanting to accept the fact that within hours I would have the missionary's mantle lifted from my shoulders.

Breaking the silence, my companion, Elder McGoon, stated matter-of-factly, "You don't want to go home, do you, Elder?"

"No," I answered, clenching my fist, "no way!" It was honestly how I felt, and even though I longed to see my family and friends, I had a hard time thinking that I would be leaving these fantastic people. They had accepted me as their own and had loved and fed me for two years; now I was leaving them, with so many errands left uncompleted.

The final night was the most difficult, as we held a testimony meeting in honor of those of us leaving. My second mission president, Keith Nielsen, and his wife, were in attendance, as were the mission office staff. A sweeter spirit I have never felt! We were all able to share our feelings and to express our love for each other. As the meeting closed, I knew that I could never walk taller than I did as a Mormon missionary in Sydney, Australia.

Departing Aussie-land

My last night was a restless one, and I tossed and turned a thousand times. My alarm at last sounded, and with a lingering shower behind me, I packed my bags into the mission van and headed for the airport.

An hour later, after giving everyone a hug good-bye, and amidst tears of sadness and joy, I waved farewell and ducked through the plane boarding gate. Before long, the plane taxied down the runway and took off, causing a bit of my heart to weep for loneliness. These people had done so much for me and had taught me so many invaluable lessons; never again would my relationship with them be the same. Truly a part of me remained in Sydney as we headed out over the ocean toward home.

Arriving at customs at the Los Angeles airport, I was greeted by our family friends, the Rogerses and the Crowders. My mom had called them and informed them of my two-hour layover, and they were kind enough to come and spend that time with me. Before long, however, it was time for me to go, and I bid them a cheery, Aussie farewell.

Finally, after a full twenty hours of travel, I heard the flight attendant announce that we were descending into the Salt Lake International Airport. I was tired of traveling, but my heart was almost in my throat as I anticipated my family and friends waiting to greet me. Still, when the plane finally stopped at our gate, I made sure the other passengers had disembarked before I stood up and gathered my belongings. Then, taking a deep breath, I walked out of the plane and into the waiting arms of those who loved me most.

After hugs and kisses from about twenty family members, and after responding to about as many television cameras, we piled into the family van and headed for home. The van still had my suggested license plate, "I'M TALL," on the back. Two hours later I laid eyes on the alfalfa field we have as our front lawn. Never had any sight been more pleasing to the eye, and what had become a distant memory now flashed before me as a new reality: home was where I belonged, and home would be an anchor—my anchor—throughout my life.

7

The 76ers and Destiny

Returning Home to Castle Dale

One of the sweetest trips of my life was driving from the airport in Salt Lake City to our home in Castle Dale. When we arrived home, we hauled my bags into the house and then grabbed a basketball and headed for the backyard. Dad and Justin thought they could take care of me, and I think they could; but when I drove breakneck for a lay-up, I slammed my elbow flush into Dad's forearm. He turned white as a sheet, and I thought for sure I had broken it. I felt just awful. So, thinking he was going into shock, we put a blanket around him and took him into town for an X ray. Luckily it wasn't broken, but it sure was a bad bruise.

After this incident, when someone asked me what would happen if Shaquille O'Neal, not my dad, came at me, I answered by saying, "I've moved cattle, and when a 2,000-pound cow is on your foot, you find a way to move it." I had gained over forty pounds in Australia, and I was splitting out the seams of my clothes. These new pounds, I knew, would be to my advantage, and I looked forward to playing against O'Neal, Patrick Ewing, David Robinson, and the rest of the big guys. I knew they could teach me a lot, and I also knew there was no reason to feel intimidated just because they had been playing for the past two years. I'd catch up, or at least I'd give it my best and die trying. For me there is just no middle ground.

One of the first things I learned upon arriving home was how much interest there was in my decision to turn pro. Sports writers from across the country were buzzing with excitement, and even though I was so out of shape I couldn't run to the mailbox, I was flattered with their words. Tom Friend of the New York *Times* even learned that upon my return, I raked my hands through my closet and found not a single T-shirt or pair of jeans that would fit. He also reported accurately that I would have to get Inga, my lifelong friend and tailor, to outfit me according to my increased bulk. It was crazy to see the things reporters picked up on, but I was used to their nose for details, so I didn't let it bother me.

Not long after our arrival, I went to visit my friend, Tracy Jeffs, and to enjoy his great spirit. I was driving my GMC that my brother, Justin, had been driving while I was in Australia. As I climbed out of the truck and embraced President Jeffs, I couldn't help but look at my truck, and say, "Boy, this thing is a pile of trash. I think when I get a little money, I'll have it restored from the inside out, and do it right this time."

"Shawn," Tracy answered, smiling, "you weren't restoring a truck back in high school. You were just in another phase of your education, learning about yourself and about completing what you set out to do."

"You sound like my dad," I replied, laughing. "He told me the other day that all those years milking the cow had little to do with milking. He said it had to do with learning follow through and stick-to-it-iveness, as well as the value of a good glass of milk."

We both laughed, and then Tracy asked, "Shawn, what was the most important thing you learned on your mission? I mean other than getting to know the Savior and to serve Him?"

"Well," I replied, almost without thinking, "the one thing I found out there is that I'm in charge of my life. I also learned not to make any major decision until I had fasted and prayed about it. It's a formula that can't fail."

"That's great, Shawn, and I couldn't agree more. I assume that, among other things, you're referring to your decision to turn pro, aren't you?"

Nodding silently, I allowed Tracy to continue with his thought.

"You know, Shawn, Elder Boyd Packer of the Quorum of the Twelve Apostles once said that important decisions shouldn't be made in a dark corner. That is, they should be made openly before the Lord. When your dad told me of your decision to leave the Y and to turn pro, I had confidence that you had made that decision on your knees, and so I haven't given it a second thought. Oh, we'll miss watching you play in Provo these next three years, but we're behind you all the way."

Tracy's words were a great comfort to me, as this decision was the most difficult of my life to this point.

Reporting My Mission

When I returned to Castle Dale, my first appointment was with my stake president, Brent Arnold. He interviewed me regarding my mission and made sure that I had returned honorably, being morally worthy to obtain what is called an "honorable release." I was also invited to speak to the stake presidency and high council, and then to speak to our entire congregation. Those experiences were fantastic, and I felt the Lord's Spirit so strongly as I told of my mission and bore testimony of my knowledge of the truths of the restored gospel of Christ.

Included in my remarks was the following: "I'm glad to be home, but I'll never forget my two-year mission. A lot of missionaries come back and say it's been the best two years of their life. But I can say it was the best two years 'for my life,' because now I know who Shawn Bradley is."

Following the services, Mom and Dad had prepared to feed the multitude of friends and family who had come to share this special day with me, and so the rest of the day was spent at our home. Mom had my homecoming open house catered, and about 250 people came to eat. It was great, and somehow I thought that a reunion in heaven would have the same emotional impact. We die and then are able to visit with all of our family and friends who have passed on before us. My only question is, what do we eat on such an occasion? Food has always been a big part of my life, and I can't comprehend the thought of not being able to eat in the afterlife.

Included in our special guests were three reporters, flying in from Denver, Philadelphia, and New York. They were actually there to interview me Monday morning, but Mom invited them to our Church services and to the home afterward, and they seemed excited to attend.

One of the highlights, or sidelights, of that afternoon was when people were out on the lawn visiting. I grabbed a basketball away from one of my cousins and let it fly toward the basket. As it sailed, I yelled, "Bradley for three," and then it swished right through the net. Talk about an answer to prayer! But, not to let the others know how lucky I had been to hit it, I simply smiled and said, "Don't mess, fellahs." We all laughed—and then headed for another round of food.

Lake Powell, a Fantastic Place to Lay Back

The day after my homecoming address in church—and after the interviews with the reporters mentioned above—our family took a long-anticipated vacation to Lake Powell with our friends the LeRoys. With all of the press being around and the pressures of the approaching NBA draft, it was the perfect hideaway for us to go to. I had been on a fast track for the previous two years, as my mission was by far the most demanding experience in my life, and now we were able to kick back, relax, and become reacquainted as a family.

I couldn't drink in enough conversation with my parents, my brother, and my sisters. They had each matured so much, and with Tasha playing basketball at the College of Eastern Utah in Price, and Justin playing in all kinds of basketball camps, it was a time we all needed and would savor in the weeks and months to come. And of course my littlest sister, Adrianne. She had grown so much and was so mature that I just wanted to talk and talk with her. She and Tasha are the most beautiful girls in the world, and I found that we had a new and refreshing level of communicating with each other. My relationship with Justin had also changed, and while he was more of a *little* brother to me before my mission, he was now a towering sixteen-year-old who really had his head on straight. I'll have to say that I couldn't have been more proud of Justin.

We had a great time, and almost before our vacation began, it had ended, and we were back in Castle Dale. I was tired, but I felt like I was really home from my mission—and the exhilaration of water skiing after two years was pure heaven!

A New One-ton King Cab Pickup

Ever since I was a little fellow, I've wanted a nice new pickup truck. When I first turned sixteen, I sort of took over my Mom's Volkswagen, and did I ever look strange driving that thing around. A kind person would say that I looked like I was driving a go-cart, while an unkind person would say that I looked like a backward-squatting grasshopper. I was only 7'2" at the time, but it was still an experience climbing in and out of that thing. I'll have to admit that there were times when I wondered about my Dad's German obsession with his VWs. He always had one, and that's just the way it was.

About that time, when I was still a sophomore in high school, my uncle gave me his old '72 GMC pickup—minus a workable engine. At the time, he told me it was mine if I could get it running. It was the same age as I was, so I pretty much figured we could work things out for each other. Well, I got the GMC running all right, but somewhere in the back of my mind I've had a secret desire to drive a brand-spanking new one right off the lot and break it in right. I had to sell a couple of cows to get the money to pay for the engine in my first one, but now things were shaping up so I could buy a new one, and was I ever excited!

Anyway, having received a signing bonus from Upper Deck, a player card manufacturing company, I was able to purchase some new civilian clothes, and more important, to buy that truck of my dreams. Again it was a GMC, but this one was decked out with a super stereo system, a sunroof, and air-conditioning. I knew I'd died and gone to heaven driving that pickup off the lot. Other than buying a few new tapes so I could learn the new songs people were singing, this was pretty much my only selfish purchase. It was so awesome—driving it was just like floating down the highway, and those first few days with it home on the ranch, I'm not sure I climbed out of it except to catch a few winks of sleep now and then.

I honestly felt that being able to get new clothes that fit and to buy my dream pickup was a great blessing from the Lord, since it took tremendous pressure off my folks, who were already tapped out financially.

A Whirlwind Tour of the NBA

Now that I was set with a truck and nice threads, I began one of the strangest dog and pony shows you could ever imagine. The top three lottery winners in the NBA—Orlando, Philadelphia, and Golden State—invited me to their cities to have me take a physical exam by their team physician so they would know whether to consider me in the approaching draft.

I've flown quite a bit in my life, yet over the next several days I felt like I became acquainted with most of the airports in the country. It was an awesome feeling, and yet very humbling, to think that these organizations would be interested in risking their entire financial fortunes on me—especially since I wouldn't work out for them. I knew what shape I was in after a two-year layoff, and so I didn't want to compromise by showing them 10 percent of who I was. They weren't happy about this decision, but they respected me for my position and settled for our getting acquainted as a potential family.

My agent, David Falk, coached me for the tour, and his perspective and encouragement made it all possible. I had come to respect his knowledge of the system, but even more I had learned that he was a man of principle and integrity and that my best interests were his concern. What I didn't know at this early hour of our relationship was how effective he was at the negotiation table. That would come. For now though, we simply got to know each other and enjoyed the whirlwind tour together.

Because of the approaching draft, there was quite a lot of hype in the press wherever I went, and the Associated Press picked up on where I was emotionally. In being interviewed in Philadelphia, I said the following:

"I'm ready to go, I want to play. I've always had the fire and desire within me. The last couple of weeks, traveling around the country, getting to meet people, I can tell that it's time to get back in there. I can feel it right now.

"As for my mission," I continued, "I have absolutely no regrets. My first baby toy was a basketball and ever since I've had a basketball in my hands. The mission was a great break for me. I loved it, the whole two years. But it also gave me a chance to develop that hunger and desire again. Basketball's not the only thing in my life. It shouldn't be in anyone's life. My religion and my family are the two most important things in my life, even though I love basketball."

In talking then about Philadelphia, and how hard the fans might be on me if I'm not an instant producer, I said, "I don't know a whole lot about Philadelphia fans. But I do know wherever you play, unless you produce you're a goat. I understand that."

When a reporter expressed skepticism about a guy who hadn't played a serious game of basketball in two years, I simply smiled and said, "I love the game so much, that kind of stuff doesn't matter. I try to take the negative and positive comments and put them in the right place."

Those words ended the interview, and before I knew it, I was on a plane for Orlando to visit the Magic. I knew I was a marked man because of my height and because I had learned good fundamental basketball, but what I wasn't prepared for was the need I would have to justify my time away from playing and my two-year mission. Still, when it kept coming up, I became increasingly peaceful, because I knew deep within that my priorities were in place and that I had put the Lord and His errand first. I don't know how a person can fail when this is his or her perspective.

I also enjoyed reading the various comments from around the country that were quoted in the national press. A couple of comments were pretty funny, like Frank Layden's, of the Utah Jazz. When I was thirteen, he had gotten me a pair of sneakers, and now he said, "I know he'll be great. He's the only 7'6" person in the world who can ride a horse." I especially enjoyed my Grandpa Wilberg's comments. He said, "Shawn was born over in Germany, and I took him a pair of cowboy boots. I was going to make a cowboy out of him, but he grew taller than the horse."

The NBA Draft in Detroit

After completing this tour, I spent a few days unwinding and working out, and I realized for the first time just how totally out of shape I was. It would take a miracle for me to get in shape for the season, but I knew that if I just lived with the pain, I could get my strength back. The good thing I had discovered was that I could still shoot a foul shot. That alone gave me hope. I knew another thing too, and that was that I would never spend two years away from the sport of basketball again, and then return to it. Still, with every wince of pain, I knew that my mission had been worth it and that I wouldn't have changed it in any way.

Before I hardly had time to breathe, I was packing my bags again, this time with the rest of my family. We had all been invited to Detroit for the annual NBA draft. I really didn't know what to expect, other than when I had visited with the first three teams to pick—Orlando, Philadelphia, and Golden State—each had appeared interested in having me play for them. The cities were totally different, as were the team owners, managers, and coaches, but I knew that I just wanted to play ball, and each team assured me that I had the potential of becoming an integral part of their team.

As we arrived at the Guest Quarters Suites Hotel, where the top NBA officials and the team organizations were waiting, I could feel my adrenaline picking up. The excitement in the air was so thick you could almost cut it with a knife, and I knew that the next hours of my life would determine a great deal of my professional destiny. The date was 30 June 1993.

In a weird way, I felt like I was a pawn and the draft had become one giant chess game. Orlando had the top pick, as they had the year before; but since they had chosen Shaq O'Neil and were building their team around him, they wouldn't need me. Both Philadelphia and Golden State had clearly announced their desire to draft me, and going into the room, I honestly felt that Orlando would pick me first, and then after Philadelphia had picked Chris Webber of Michigan State, Golden State would take Anfernee Hardaway. Orlando would then trade me for Anfernee. This would mean that I would end up with Coach Don Nelson at Golden State, Chris would be in

Philadelphia, and Anfernee in Orlando to complement Shaq from the guard line.

Anyway, here we were, sitting around a table in the Palace with my agent, David Falk, thinking that the chess game would begin and that after three moves, I would land permanently in the Bay area playing for Coach Nelson. What we didn't know was how badly Philadelphia wanted me and how good they were at bluffing with their chess move. At the last minute they threatened to take Anfernee second, after I had been taken by Orlando. They knew how badly Orlando wanted him to complement the "Shaq Attack!" So with this last-minute threat (which was disclosed to Orlando literally sixty seconds before the draft began), Orlando knew they couldn't take the chance of losing Anfernee. As a result, when they made their announcement, they chose Webber, knowing that Golden State would take Anfernee third and then they could make their trade.

Commissioner David Stern finally stepped to the podium and made the announcement of Chris Webber going to the Orlando Magic as their number one pick. Everyone clapped and whistled, congratulating Chris as he put on an Orlando Magic cap and was then interviewed. When the applause finally died down, Commissioner Stern took the second envelope, opened it, and announced that I was being drafted by the Philadelphia 76ers. At that moment I felt unbelievable excitement, and again the applause erupted. I was in a bit of a daze, and as I walked up to the rostrum, I could see what seemed like a thousand flash cameras going off.

Finally, after what seemed like forever, the pandemonium died down, and I was likewise interviewed. My heart was pumping a hundred miles an hour, I was so excited, but deep within myself, I felt a strange, peaceful calm. One reporter had called out to me, asking if I was disappointed in not being taken first, but to me the question was absurd. I wasn't concerned about the financial ramifications of either pick, or the prestige of going first versus second or third. I had hoped only that the right doors would be opened for me and that I would be placed in the city and organization that I could make the greatest contribution to. I felt a sense of peace that I had come to recognize whispering to my spirit that this was *right* for me.

Actually, because I hadn't played for two years and had only played collegiate ball for one year at that, I felt honored to even be in the presence of the other athletes. I knew that I was a giant gamble and that any team taking me was taking the financial gamble of a lifetime by drafting me. I knew my work ethic, and I also felt that my skill level would return; but still, as I tried to look at things from their position, I knew the risk they were taking.

Later that night, after I had retired to my bed, I found myself looking up into the darkness, almost not believing that my life's dream of being drafted into the National Basketball Association was at long last being realized. For years, it had seemed like the top of the summit and that if I were ever fortunate enough to climb that high, then I would have arrived. Now, though, as I gazed out into the darkness of my hotel room, my eyes could almost see new peaks and horizons ahead of me. At this moment I realized that I had perhaps climbed to the alpine meadows, thinking there were no greater mountains to climb. But there certainly were, and with newly gained perspective, I knew that I had only just begun my personal and professional ascent.

My thoughts turned then to my Church mission in Australia and the unparalleled growth and mountains I had climbed in service to my God. Just when I had felt like I had accomplished all that there was to do as a missionary, new horizons with unanticipated challenges would open before me. Thank goodness, I thought, that my parents had always taught me to look ahead and to approach each new moment of my life with confidence, knowing that the Lord would give me the strength to do my best if I but did my part. Those ideas seemed so basic now, and yet they rang ever so true in my mind.

My thoughts reverted then back to Castle Dale and to my sophomore basketball coach, J.R. Nelson. He was one of the greatest men I had known and had shown such confidence in me and in my future. Thank goodness, I thought, for the J.R. Nelsons of my life, men who had lived with integrity and greatness and who knew how to instill it in others.

These were my thoughts as I finally closed my eyes and fell asleep. And somewhere between the zones of sleep and consciousness, I saw myself dribbling the length of the floor, wearing my new 76er uniform, then gliding toward the basket and slamming the ball through while all of my new friends in Philadelphia (as well as my old friends in Utah) shouted and whistled their approval. The feeling was simply awesome, and one that I hoped to repeat in the real world as the season would begin.

Kicking Back at the Ranch

One of the great moments since my return from my mission was hopping into my truck and heading over to where my Grandpa Wilberg and my uncles and cousins were branding calves. As always, it was a family affair, and my little sister Adrianne was out on her horse, rounding up the calves for the brand.

By the time I arrived, the others had already eaten a big spread of food over at my Aunt Sandra's and were back in the corral, branding away like there was no tomorrow. They welcomed me without stopping what they were doing, so I assumed my usual spot near the head of the calf being branded. My job had always been to use a needle to inject serum into the shoulder of the calf so it could be immunized against seven types of diseases common to livestock. The main immunization is for blackleg.

In addition to branding and giving the calves the serum, we also notched one ear, tagged the other, and dehorned them— all for the purposes of identification. If we didn't dehorn them, they would likely grow up with an "attitude," so this helped keep their ornery nature from coming out. The other thing we did for the calves was separate them out, depending on whether we were going to put them on the east mountain or in Joe's Valley to the west.

One of our constant worries in cattle raising was calving, or the birth process. The calves would often get their legs caught inside the mother, and we'd take a specially designed rope with a loop on one end and a wooden handle on the other. We'd have to put our hand up inside the mother, loop the rope around the calf's legs, and then pull it out. We called this apparatus a come-along, and with two or three people helping, it would usually work.

At other times, a cow would eat more of something than it

should and become bloated. We'd save the cow's life by using a cut-off piece of hose and some kitchen oil. We'd hold the cow down, then stick the hose all the way down its throat until the hose reached the stomach. We'd then pour oil down the hose, and before long it would set off a reaction causing the cow to belch, allowing the gas to escape out through its mouth. I tell you, we knew better than to stand in front of that hose.

Perhaps this would be the moment to relate just one incident with my little sister Tasha. When we were little, she found a rotten goose egg and got a little too close to it. They're pretty fragile, and this one exploded all over her. Mom was there, as was I, and we both ran in opposite directions away from her. She just stood there crying and smelling awful. Mom finally got the hose and sprayed her down so we could stand to be by her. I don't think she ever got close to a rotten egg again after that experience.

Getting back to my day of branding with Grandpa Wilberg, he and I had been looking forward to sharing this time together for two years, and it was great to finally be working back at his side. Something unexpected happened in midafternoon, as he picked my dad's brand from the red coals and branded a particular calf.

"Well," he said, smiling up at me, "there he is, Shawn, the first calf of your own herd. Your very own Bar-B-Bar brand." Dad had used the brand for as long as I could remember, and it felt good to think that I could now use it to begin my own herd.

I was dumbfounded as Grandpa spoke, and so not knowing how to respond, I allowed him to continue. "I figured it was about time you started your own herd, Shawn, and if you need me to, I'll sort of keep an eye on it and help you get it off and running."

"Wow, Grandpa!" I exclaimed, seeing in my mind's eye an entire herd with my own brand proudly displayed on the left rear flank. "I'm not really sure what to say, but thanks . . . thanks a million!"

He gave me a big smile, and as my uncles and cousins all looked on, I knew I was the luckiest guy in the whole world. Nobody could have a granddad as great as mine. After spending years helping him with his cattle, he was now thanking me by giving me a start for my very own herd. Right then I couldn't wait to get married and have kids so they could learn the lessons of ranching from my knee, just as I had learned from Grandpa's. It was a moment I will always remember.

With Rob at Our Cabin in Joe's Valley

A few days before leaving for Philadelphia, one of my truest of friends, Rob Kimmel, dropped by with his folks, Jim and Betty, on their way back from a family outing at Lake Powell. His fiancée, Michelle, was with them, and we laughed and joked together on the sofa in our basement. When it was time for them to continue back to their home in Provo, I asked Rob if he would consider staying on the ranch with me. He knew that I was under quite a bit of pressure in my life, and he said that he would. So, saying good-bye to Michelle and his folks, he and I jumped into my old pickup and headed down the lane (I knew we would be gully hopping over some pretty rough terrain, and I didn't want to scratch up my new truck). We spent the evening winding through the foothills, getting stuck, and in general having the time of our lives. It was just what I needed—time to clear my head and be a kid again, doing crazy things.

The next morning, after working out at the gym, Rob and I waved good-bye to the folks and headed west up Straight Canyon. It was actually crooked as a dog's hind leg, which is why I think they called it Straight Canyon. Anyway, we were on our way to our family's cabin, in Joe's Valley, and I couldn't wait to get there. As we crested up out of the canyon, I shared memories of the lake and of the time I had hunted and bagged my first and only buck in the nearby mountains.

Turning then to Rob, I asked if he wanted the greatest bacon cheeseburger and fries of his life. He just smiled and licked his lips, and seconds later we wheeled into the Sportsman's Lodge. When we entered, the owner was behind the grill, and so we ordered up my favorite.

The burger and fries were great! As we left, I told the owner good-bye and that he could expect us to be back in three or four hours for a second round. My *excuse* was that I had to gain weight, but my *reason* is that I can never get enough of those burgers and that I would really miss eating them in the weeks and months to come.

Before long we arrived at our cabin. While we were checking things out, we climbed the ladder into the loft and then walked out on the balcony.

"You know, Rob," I reminisced back to glory days at the cabin, "this valley has been Grandpa's for years, and it's the closest to heaven I've ever gotten."

"It is beautiful, Shawn," he answered, "and if I remember right, your family's property extends quite a ways to the north."

"Yeah, all the way up to that fence on the other end of the meadow. Those cows are ours, and I think Grandpa is bringing up some more this afternoon."

"You think you'll ever build yourself a cabin up here, Shawn?"

"Sure do. Grandpa told me to just pick out my spot, and it's mine. He's so giving, I can hardly believe it. I just hope that I can live as unselfishly as he has. Then I know I'll have done things right."

We talked for some time, enjoying the comradarie that is central to our friendship. Concluding our conversation, we wandered down through the meadow toward my truck. Before long, we were winding our way up out of our property, once again thinking about cheeseburgers and fries at the Lodge. Neither of us could wait!

Arriving in Philadelphia

Two days later, Rob and I headed for Provo, and then to the airport in Salt Lake City. As we said good-bye, I knew that somehow things would never quite be the same for us. Oh, our friendship would stretch into the eternities, as all true friendships do, but with the new direction I was taking, our time together would become limited and our loyalties would of course be with our companions, and with our new families. It was a lonely thought, but I knew that Rob would always be there for me, as would my other friends, and that when things became difficult, we could always make contact and receive the support and encouragement each needed.

As my plane left the ground and headed for Philadelphia, I offered a silent prayer for safety and thanked the Lord for Rob and for the others who had rallied around me in my life. I knew that a person was fortunate to have a few true friends throughout life, and Rob was certainly that for me.

Arriving in Philly for Good

Not long after my plane touched down in this historic city, my agent, David Falk, informed me that the mayor of Philadelphia, Mr. Ed Rendell, wanted to meet me. I was surprised by this request because it was I who wanted to meet him! But we did meet, and during the course of our conversation, he said something that surprised and humbled me all in the same breath. He told me that he expected me to change the spirit of Philadelphia from one of criticism and derision to one of kindness and supportiveness. I'm not really sure what he meant, but I know the press there has had a way of maligning professional athletes—sort of chewing them up and spitting them out.

I appreciated Mayor Rendell's confidence in me. With the conviction that this is the city where I needed to begin my professional basketball career, I accepted his challenge. After all, the only way I have been taught to treat others is with a gentle sensitivity to them as individuals, as the Savior did. Actually, I've found that it's easier and takes less energy to be nice to people than it does to live with anger and a spirit of being judgmental.

Signing My Contract

After spending three weeks in Philadelphia, working out and returning my strength and playing skills, the day of signing my contract finally arrived. Because of the unique situation of me being in Philadelphia and in training without a contract, as well as the positive press reviews I had received (not to mention the excitement that the owners and management had in having me on their team), the stage was set for a speedy contract negotiation. With my attorney's incredible skill, my contract with the Sixers was completed in one day.

From the owner's perspective, as well as from mine, the contract was more than fair.

I invited Mom and Dad to come to the signing, so they flew out from Utah and received a warm welcome in Philadelphia. I feel it is important to include them in my life at every step of the way, and it was fantastic seeing them again! They are, without question, the reason I am where I am today, and I certainly want to share my life and good fortunes with them. I was also excited for them to meet Jim and Tammy Engebretsen, who had opened their home for me to live in until I found something more permanent. Jim is the bishop of the singles ward here in Philly, and with their five young daughters running around to keep the excitement up, the home had become the perfect place for me to stay. Mom and Dad were coming to stay with us for a few days, so I felt great.

The signing of my contract was held at the Sixers' office, near where they play ball. The press conference would then be held at the Guest Quarters Suites, by the airport. They're great folks there, and from what I've been told, they were going to do it up big for the press conference, announcing that I was now officially a 76er.

As we left the hotel, Dad was the first to speak. Taking a deep breath, he said, "Shawn, you'll never know how excited we are to share this moment with you. We couldn't be more proud of the way you're handling yourself."

"Thanks, Dad," I answered, feeling every bit as excited as I ever did before playing a big game. "My head's swimming, actually, and yet I am humbled beyond words with the opportunity the Lord has given me."

"Honey," Mom interjected, "your grandparents, aunts and uncles, cousins, and especially Tasha, Adrianne, and Justin wanted us to give you their love. In fact, the whole town, for that matter. You'll never know how much support you have from back home that things will work out for you."

"They are working out, believe me. It's a bit overwhelming, actually," I answered, hearing my old Australian accent come out of my mouth. "But I honestly don't feel any different. I'm just me, with a lot of opportunity to do some good. Everyone I meet asks me if I feel any different, now that I've signed a contract that is so staggering."

"Do you, Shawn?" Dad asked, I think wanting some reassurance.

"Well, in a way I do, although not in a selfish way. Oh, I'm thrilled that I can build you guys a new home and help out in ways that will make your life more comfortable. Also, I really want to help a friend who has high medical expenses as a result of her kidney disease. On top of that, I have to say that I do enjoy having a truck big enough to comfortably sit in when I'm going someplace, and with a great stereo sound system. But, to answer your question, Dad, I do feel different in that I suddenly feel responsible for wisely stewarding a whole lot of money. I don't see it as mine, really, but as just mine to take care of so that I can help make the world a better place."

"Well," Mom added, "your friend, Steve Young, has warned you about not allowing it to change who you are."

"He's done a lot more than that," I answered, smiling. "He has set up his foundation for helping young people, and his focus is on others rather than on himself. I never want to be different than who you've raised me to be; I just want to play ball and let the youth out there know that we can accomplish anything we set our minds to, even without compromising our values."

Following the events of the evening, we retired to my room, where just the three of us visited. Sometime later, long after they had retired to their room, I lay on my bed, gazing blankly at the dimly lit ceiling. The events leading up to this day, as well as the actual experience itself, was nothing short of a miracle, and I could hardly believe they were happening to me. But then, remembering a similar quiet moment in my missionary apartment in Australia, I breathed a sigh of relief. The events were inevitable, really, and somehow I wished the day would never end.

A Semi "R & R" with My Folks

Following the signing of my contract, my folks and I were pretty much left to ourselves to enjoy the weekend together. They wanted to see as many historical sites as possible, and so while I worked out, they cut a pretty wide swath through Philadelphia.

We were also able to spend some quality time together, and it felt great being with them. I introduced them to a new friend, Annette Evertsen, whom I had met at church, and the four of us had some good times together. Annette was originally from Salt Lake City, but she had recently returned from serving a Spanish-speaking mission in Ft. Lauderdale, Florida, and was now working as a nanny in Philly. She had worked for the same family prior to serving a mission, and they had liked her so much that they talked her into returning for one last summer.

At any rate, the four of us swam in the pool where she lived and totally enjoyed being together. I was thrilled with how well Annette hit it off with my folks, too, since she had become my closest friend in Philly, and I wanted Mom and Dad to feel of her character and her support.

Finally, knowing that he either had to get back to work at the medical center or be fired, Dad made flight arrangements, and he and Mom flew back to Utah. I knew I would miss them, just as I had done while in Australia, but I felt close to them spiritually, and I knew they would be fine. Besides, I had to get my new pickup truck out to Philadelphia, and I had a hunch that I could talk them into returning in two or three weeks for that purpose.

They did return, too, in the middle of August. And with them came my sisters, Tasha and Adrianne. They drove that one-ton duelly pickup clear across the country, seeing sights along the way. When they arrived, they were exhausted, but by morning we were running around, totally enjoying ourselves. It was the first time my sisters had been here, and it was great seeing them learn about Philadelphia. They were also able to drive down to Washington, D.C., and to catch a quick glimpse of the nation's political hub there.

The family stayed for five days, and on the second day, my little brother, Justin, flew in to join us. Well, he wasn't really *little*, at 6'8", but I've always called him that. He's always been supportive and excited with my successes. Now it's my turn, and because his basketball skills are developed beyond mine when I was about to enter my junior year of high school, I have great hopes for his future on the hardcourt!

The highlight of our trip, for me, was our jaunt into New York City with my now girlfriend, Annette, and with Tammy

Engebretsen. Mom, Dad, and Tasha came along, and even though Adrianne and Justin had to stay home for lack of room in my truck, the rest of us went to see *Phantom of the Opera* on Broadway. It was our first live Broadway production, and we all loved it.

My days with Justin and Tasha turned out to be even better than we had hoped for. Justin worked out with me, and in between our hours at the gym, we saw the city, went to movies, had fun with Annette and other friends, and in general had a week together that strengthened our relationship—bonding us even deeper at an adult level. It was a tender, personal time for us.

I hated to take Justin and Tasha to the airport when our visit came to an end, but I knew that they had lots to do in getting ready for school. So we gave each other giant hugs, and said our farewells. It was fantastic to have the love and support I had from them and from Adrianne. They've stood patiently by me during my moments in the limelight, and without being jealous they have been my greatest supporters. I love them for it. I just hope I can be as involved with them and their lives and that I can give them the same support they've given me. They're the greatest!

The 76ers Acquire Moses Malone

The month of August continued, and in addition to my regimentation of 7,200 calories a day, I found myself gaining strength and getting the feel of the ball back in my hands. Then one day, while working out, Coach Freddie Carter came to me and told me the 76ers had just inked a deal to have Moses Malone come back on the team. I knew this had been in the works, and was I ever excited! I knew that at age 38, Malone, who began his pro career nineteen years ago with the Utah Stars of the American Basketball Association, would be a fantastic mentor. He had played for the Sixers in the mid-80s, and had helped them win the NBA championship in '83. Even though it had been seven years since he had played for the team, he would be a tremendous addition to our team. I was just two years old, playing in my sandbox in Provo, when Moses began his pro career forty-five miles to the north. Now we were to be together, working to make me into the most effective player possible.

When Moses was interviewed about his new teacher role on our team, he said, "[Shawn] is going to be a great ballplayer, but you just can't say, 'Do it now.' I'm looking forward to working with the young guy. I'm looking forward to helping him. Above all, I want to show Shawn that no one is going to be his friend on the court. My goal is to help develop him into an imposing center with a 'mean' attitude."

I appreciated Moses' candidness, and I also agreed with the comment made by our general manager, Jim Lynam, who was quoted as saying that Malone was brought back to Philadelphia to allow me to learn firsthand from one of the great centers who ever played the game.

In considering my new profile as the nucleus for our team of the future, I was surprised when *USA Today* ran a feature article on me on 3 August. In the article, they outlined my daily food intake:

Shawn Bradley's 7,200-Calorie Day

Beefing up for the NBA is a tall order for Shawn Bradley. What he must consume in a typical day:

Breakfast—Two eggs, two bagels with cream cheese and jelly, 12 ounces of whole milk, cup of fruit, slice of whole-wheat bread with peanut butter.

Midmorning Snack—Snickers bar, one pint of Gatorade, 1,000-calorie high-carbohydrate milk shake.

Lunch—Barbecued chicken breast, salad with ranch dressing, vegetable, cup of pretzels, cup of potatoes, 16 ounces of orange juice.

Mid-afternoon Snack—Two Snickers bars, or two additional 1,000-calorie shakes.

Dinner—Barbecued beef filet, corn on the cob with butter, salad with ranch dressing, vegetable, potato salad, pasta salad, 16 ounces of orange juice.

Evening Snack—Bagel with cream cheese, 20 ounces of orange juice.

Movie Munchies—Large box of Milk Duds, Twizzlers, buttered popcorn, 16-ounce soft drink.

Source: Pat Croce

As you can see, the Sixers have obviously demonstrated a lot of confidence and trust in me. I want to work hard to understand some of the things I need to do to be the best. As long as I do that, everybody will be happy. As further quoted in this article, I'm just a twenty-one-year-old farm kid from central Utah who happens to love basketball. When asked in that article how people respond to my height, I told the reporter that most of the time people swear. Then I mentioned that one time recently I was walking in a mall, and a friend I was with said, "You know, Shawn, you cause the most swearing. Then they ask how tall you are." He was right, of course, and I truthfully don't mind. But it would be nice if people didn't have to cuss to express themselves.

As a final note, the reporter asked me about my Mormon religion. I was quoted correctly when I suggested that the biggest misconception is that we're fanatic Bible-bashing people out to destroy people's religion and convert them. From my experience, we're out there to try to share some things that we feel make our lives better—and we make ourselves available to anyone who wants to listen. If a person isn't interested, we'll graciously give them the opportunity to say no, more than one time. But above all, we respect the views of others.

And so, as fall approaches, and as my life in Philadelphia becomes increasingly complex, I take great pride in how I'm adjusting. Life as a 76er is certainly full time and more intense than anything I've experienced. I see myself on a second mission now, one that is exhausting and exhilarating all in the same breath, and yet one that is totally fun! My goal is to make an immediate contribution to the success of our franchise, and then to build upon this year's experience in taking us all the way to the NBA championship. After all, could I be content with less? No way. *NO WAY!!*

8

What I'm All About

My True Beginnings

For those of you who are not of my faith and yet have been kind enough to allow me to share my beliefs, I sincerely thank you. Still, I feel you deserve a more thorough explanation. In the concluding pages of this book, then, I would like to put my religion in its proper perspective so that I won't have cheated you by telling you just part of my story.

To do this, allow me to take you on a brief but exciting journey into upstate New York. The year is 1830, and a fourteen-year-old farm boy named Joseph Smith has just been reading the book of James in the New Testament. There is a great deal of religious fervor in that area, and while his family have mostly joined the Presbyterian church, he has become partial to the Methodist faith.

On this particular spring morning, while tromping through the field toward a grove of trees to the west of the farmland he and his family have been clearing, he reflects upon the words of James, wherein he learned that if anyone lacked wisdom, he could ask of God, and this wisdom would be given him. In the innocence of youth, Joseph really believed that he could learn which faith he should join so that he could be true to his religious beliefs.

At any rate, after arriving in the grove of trees, young Joseph knelt down and offered a humble prayer—the first time in his life that he had attempted to pray vocally. To Joseph's utter astonishment, he found himself engulfed in a pillar of light, exactly over his head, that seemed brighter than the noonday sun. As this light rested upon him, Joseph saw, standing above him in the air, two personages, whose brightness and glory defied all description. One of these personages, while pointing to the other, called Joseph by name, and said, "This is My Beloved Son. Hear Him."

I have tried to imagine myself in Joseph's position at that moment as he was struggling to comprehend who was appearing to him and just what was unfolding before him. He soon realized, however, that his understanding was increasing by the second. The personage who had just been introduced then spoke, telling Joseph that he was none other than Jesus Christ, the Savior of the world. This must have been especially perplexing to Joseph, since he had been taught that God the Father and Jesus Christ, were one being with the Holy Ghost. But here he was seeing two distinct beings, one of whom instructed Joseph that he should join none of the churches under consideration.

Joseph was then told that the Savior's church organization, the one Jesus had established while on the earth, as Paul described in his letter to the Ephesians, had been taken from the earth. Christ told Joseph that it was his charge to assist the Savior in having this same church *restored*, or brought back to the earth.

What Joseph didn't know that morning, as this almost incomprehensible vision closed before him, was that it would be another ten years before he would be given the power to restore the Savior's church. In the meanwhile, he was to have some additional heavenly manifestations that would literally change for him the face of Christianity as the world then knew it.

Without going into great detail, Joseph's second visit from a heavenly messenger occurred one night, three years after the Father and Son had appeared to him. He was alone in his humble bedroom, and after retiring to bed, he was astonished to again see the heavens open and a man dressed in exquisite white robes descend and stand before him. This man announced himself as Moroni, a prophet who had lived upon the earth some 1,400 years earlier.

Moroni told the seventeen-year-old Joseph that a sacred record had been kept by his people and that Moroni's father, Mormon, had abridged this record upon gold plates. Joseph then learned that these plates were deposited in a hill just two miles to the east of his farm and that it was his responsibility to prepare himself to translate these golden plates so that the world could have a second witness, along with the Bible, that Jesus really was the Savior of the world. He told Joseph that the plates actually contained a thousand-year journal of a prophet and his descendants, who left Jerusalem in 600 B.C. They traveled across the ocean to the Americas, and here grew into the Indian nations of North, Central, and South America. Joseph also learned that this Moroni was the last of these prophets, whose job it was to hide the plates up until the hour that the Lord would have them brought back out of the ground and translated for the benefit of man in these last days.

Moroni returned to Joseph four more times during the next twenty-four hours, the last time on the hill where the plates had been hid. Joseph was able to handle the ancient record at that time, along with a breastplate and set of interpreters, which Moroni called the Urim and Thummim. He told Joseph that this Urim and Thummim had been used by the ancient prophets to obtain revelation and to assist in translating languages. In my studies, I have found seven biblical references to these ancient interpreters.

In continuing, Joseph was visited by this angel Moroni at least nine times over the next four years—receiving instructions that would assist him in translating this ancient sacred record. When Joseph finally began translating, he had only about sixty-five days in which to complete his work. But, complete it he did, and it was finally published as the Book of Mormon in 1830, just weeks before the Savior's church was restored to the earth. It was then placed next to the Holy Bible, to be used as a supportive document testifying that Jesus Christ was not simply a great prophet, as some believe, but that he literally atoned for our sins while in the Garden of Gethsemane and upon the cross at Calvary.

In sharing this brief history, I would be remiss if I didn't mention two other heavenly visits Joseph had while translating the golden plates. The first occurred 15 May 1829, as John the Baptist came to Joseph and his associate, Oliver Cowdery, and conferred upon their heads the Priesthood of Aaron, thus giving them the authority to act for God in baptizing others. This visitation had been recorded by the Apostle Matthew, in chapter 17 of his Gospel, verses 11 through 13. John the Baptist was even mentioned there by name, as the Savior said that he would come in the latter days to help restore all things.

Shortly after this experience, the great Apostles Peter, James, and John also returned to the earth and placed their hands upon Joseph's head, giving him the higher Melchizedek Priesthood, which included the authority of the Apostles. Thus Joseph had the ability to confer the Holy Ghost upon others and to ordain others to the same higher priesthood, including a quorum of Twelve Apostles, just as the Church had as its foundation during Christ's ministry.

What This Means to Me

As I mentioned in chapter 3, when I reached the age of eight, my father took me down into the waters of baptism, and in the same manner that Christ was baptized, *and by the same authority*, I became a member of the Church of Jesus Christ. This day was the happiest day for me, as I was then able to receive the gift of the Holy Ghost, again under the hands of my father. It also meant that I could then prepare to receive the Aaronic Priesthood at age twelve.

When I approached my nineteenth birthday, as I have also mentioned, I was then able to receive the higher Melchizedek Priesthood and to be ordained to the office of an elder in the Church. This allowed me to represent the Lord as a missionary in Australia and to be counted as one of his trusted sons. I am still overwhelmed with this sacred trust.

God's Greatest Gift

As mentioned above, after being baptized, my dad and others placed their hands upon my head and, using their priesthood, gave me the gift of the Holy Spirit. This gift means that as long as I live worthily, I am entitled to the constant guidance and direction of the Holy Ghost—whose stewardship it is to be a revelator, a comforter, and a spirit of truth.

In the fourteen years that I have enjoyed this gift, I have learned loneliness when I have erred and transgressed a given commandment. I have also experienced joy beyond words when I have made a correct decision based upon impressions of this same Spirit. While there have been literally hundreds of times that I have relied upon promptings from the Holy Ghost, there have been three times that I have literally seen my life changed as I have responded to these whisperings. These were (1) my decision to attend BYU, even though other colleges presented possibilities of higher profile for my potential in the NBA; (2) my decision to serve the Lord for two years as a missionary, knowing the risk such a course would place on my potential as a basketball player; and (3) my untimely decision to not return to the Y, but to go immediately from my mission into the NBA. You could say that not one of these decisions made any rational sense and that each went against clear and widespread logic. But I knew the source of the impressions, and I also knew that if I was to be true to this gift that I had received at age eight, I could take no other course. I just hope that I will always have the personal integrity to continue to follow these same promptings and that I will not allow the enticements of the world to change who I am.

My Ultimate Dream

Now that I've taken you to upstate New York, let me take you west, to the great state of Utah. About twenty-five miles due west of my home in Castle Dale is the small rural town of Manti. I have mentioned the high school, the Manti Templars, earlier, and how I have enjoyed competing against their teams. But this city stands as something far greater than high school athletics. For you of other faiths, this quaint farming community would likely be unknown, but for you who are Latter-day Saints, it is known as one of nearly fifty locations that stand unique among all others. For there, on the crest of a knoll, is a stately, century-old structure known as the Manti Temple.

Ever since I can remember, I have been aware of this beautiful, giant edifice; and I have longed for the day when I could enter it with my bride-to-be and there be married. From what I have been taught, I know that if I am morally worthy, I will be granted the blessing of marrying my sweetheart not just for our time here on the earth but for all eternity. That makes sense to me, as I can't imagine either of us investing a lifetime into a relationship that will conclude the day one of us died.

But this is getting ahead of my story. Let me back up two thousand years, and then come forward in time, sharing what I have learned about the beginning of temples here upon the earth.

A Brief Historical Sketch

At the time of Christ, the great Temple of Solomon was being rebuilt for the third time. It had originally been constructed about 1,000 B.C., and sacred priesthood ordinances had been performed within its walls. It was finally destroyed a third and last time in the great Roman wars of A.D. 70-71, when over a million Christians were tortured and put to death.

In Our Day

The LDS church was just a year old in 1831 when the Prophet Joseph Smith received instructions from the Lord to build a sacred temple. The temple was completed in 1836 in Kirtland, Ohio. The early Mormons were driven west, settling first in Missouri, and then in Nauvoo, Illinois. In this latter place a second temple was built.

Finally, after being invited to leave the State of Illinois, the early Mormons began their trek westward, walking over 1,500 miles until they reached the valley of the Great Salt Lake. Once here, Brigham Young began a third temple on the ten acres that have become known as historic Temple Square in Salt Lake City. Because it took forty years to complete this building, three other temples were completed first, the third of which being the Manti Temple I mentioned earlier. Now, over 150 years after the first LDS temple was completed in Ohio, the 47th temple was recently completed in San Diego, California.

I have always appreciated the teachings of my parents as they have instilled within my heart a desire to keep God's commandments so that one day, when I have found the girl of my dreams, I will be worthy to walk with her into one of these historic, holy temples. That dream told me that this girl would have served a mission, even as I had. It also told me that she would hold sacred the same values I did, that her spirit would be beautiful, and that her knowledge of the gospel would be the keystone in rearing our children.

On Saturday morning, 25 September 1993, this most precious dream became a reality. With our families as witnesses to our greatest moment ever, Annette Evertsen and I were sealed together as husband and wife for the rest of our lives—as well as for all eternity!

In Conclusion

As I thumb back through the pages of my life, I hope that I have represented myself and others fairly, and that by sharing my joys and successes, I haven't done so in a boasting manner. Every day when I awaken, I find myself discovering more and more about me and you and the world in which we live. While there are a vocal few who seek to destroy this world or to take that which isn't theirs, still I have found that most people are good, Godfearing folks who simply want to do good without imposing on others.

From my limited experience, I have found that there are basically two different types of people in the world. First is the person who walks around with a mirror in one hand so they can enjoy looking at themselves. This person also has a lamp in their other hand so that others can see him and adore him. In essence, they are walking around being illuminated by the lamp of their own self-importance.

The second kind of person is one who also carries a mirror.

But, instead of having it directed back at themselves, they are putting their arms around others and allowing these others to get a good look at themselves and then learn to more fully love themselves. In other words, they are people builders, rather than self-promoters. This second kind of person also carries a lamp, but instead of manufacturing their own light, they are illuminated by the light of Christ.

It is this second type of person that I want to become. While I know that I have been given the gift of height and the gift of athletic coordination, I can't allow myself to focus on that. I really don't want to have myself as my theme. I want to use my Godgiven talents and abilities to serve others and to lift their eyes so they can more fully understand their own potential. So many great people have taken a chisel to me and have hammered away, hoping to sculpt me into someone useful to society. This means someone who excels in efforts far greater than a slam dunk, a sky hook, or a blocked shot. It means someone who uses money as a stewardship and who spends life quietly reaching into the lives and hearts of others—being sensitive to their needs and then helping to meet those needs.

I'm enough of an idealist to believe that each of us—regardless of our race, religion, or economic situation—has the potential for greatness. Each of us has been born with what I have been taught is the Light of Christ, which is the ability to discern our own gifts and to desire to do good. It is my sincere hope that by sharing who I am and by exposing my innermost feelings and beliefs, you will want to join hands with me in making our world a truly better place.

A final thought: in 348 B.C. the great philosopher Plato died. His protégé, Socrates, was invited to give the eulogy at his grave site. Among other things, Socrates said these words: "Plato showed us by his life, that to be happy is to be good." If I have made any statement in this book, or with my life to this point, it is my desire to live life to its fullest, which I think can only be done by being good. While I am working to overcome weaknesses every day that I live, still my intent is there, and because of this I am happy.

And so, as you see me playing with a large orange ball with other gifted athletes, and perspiration is dripping off my chin, know that deep inside me, there is peace. Oh, there is a fire, to be sure—a fire deep inside that won't allow me to be content with past accomplishments. But above all, there is peace, and there is joy. That, to me, is the ultimate reward for standing tall.

Shawn Bradley's Honors and Accomplishments

Growing Up

1982 One-on-one 4-H competition: 2nd place
1983 One-on-one 4-H competition: 1st place
1984 Attended two Jazz summer camps with Coach Bob Starr
1985 Attended BYU summer camp
1985 Earned Eagle Scout award
1986 Junior high championship: 8th grade
1987 Junior high championship: 9th grade
1987 Inducted into National Junior Honors Society
1987 Jazz summer camp, one-on-one competition: 1st place
1987 AAU Tournament (Salt Lake City): 2nd place
1987 AAU Tournament (Seattle, Washington, Junior Olympics): 5th place
1987 BCI Tournament (Phoenix, Arizona): 2nd place
1987 AAU Tournament (Las Vegas, Nevada): 5th place

1988—Sophomore Year

Season averages: 13 points, 7 rebounds, 6 blocked shots
Class president

Inducted into National Honors Society
Utah 2-A State Basketball Tournament: Emery High, 3rd place
Deseret News all-state team
Salt Lake *Tribune* all-state team
2-A region tournament: All-tournament team
AAU (Salt Lake City): Salt Lake Team, 1st place; MVP of
    tournament
Utah Summer Games, region play-off: 2nd place
Utah Summer Games, bronze medal
BYU summer camp: All-star
UVCC team camp (Orem, Utah): Emergy High, camp cham-
    pions
Nike-ABCD camp (New Jersey): Attended
BCI Tournament (Phoenix, Arizona): 2nd place

1989—Junior Year

Season averages: 26 points, 13 rebounds, 9 blocked shots
Class president
Holiday Classic: All-tournament team
Utah Region 10 tournament: Emery High, 1st place; MVP of
    tournament
Utah 2-A State Tournament: Emery High, state champions
UVCC Team Camp: Emery High, 2nd place
Parade Magazine: 3rd Team All-American
Gatorade Circle of Champions: Utah High School Basketball
    Player of Year
Salt Lake *Tribune:* All-state, MVP
Deseret News: All-state, MVP
AAU (Las Vegas, Nevada): All-tournament team
Utah Summer Games, region: 1st place, gold medal
Utah Summer Games, state: 2nd place, silver medal
Fred Roberts Camp (Salt Lake City): Assistant
Nike-ABCD Camp (Princeton University, New Jersey):
    Attended
Los Angeles Reebok Slam-N-Jam Tournament: Utah Rags Team,
    5th place
Las Vegas Tournament: Utah Rags Team, 3rd place
Member Utah all-stars team, Beat Soviet Junior Olympic Team
    in Salt Lake City
Utah Naismith Award

Utah Mr. Basketball
Emery High: Lettered in basketball and baseball

1990—Senior Year

Season averages: 25 points, 17 rebounds, 9 blocked shots
Class vice president
Peerhelper officer
Emery High: Lettered in basketball and golf
School musicals: *Once upon a Mattress; Sir Studley the Knight*
Top 20 in *USA Today*
Who's Who Among American High School Students
Utah Chapter of National M.S. Society: 1989 Outstanding
    High School Male Athlete
Street and Smith magazine: 2nd Team All-American
Dick Vitale: 1st Team All-American
Basketball Times: Listed as one of top three centers
All-Star Sports: Listed no. 1 in "Top Super Six"
Parade: 2nd Team All-American
USA Today: One of "Top Five"
Salt Lake *Tribune:* All-state, MVP
Deseret News: All-state, MVP
All-region team: MVP
McDonald's All-American Game (Indiana): MVP

1990–91—Freshman Year, BYU

Season statistics: 187 of 361 field goals made (.518 F.G.%)
    1 of 1 three-point field goals made
    128 of 185 free throws made (.692 F.T.%)
    262 rebounds (7.7 per game)
    503 points made (14.8 per game)
Associated Press: Honorable Mention All-American
All-District Seven (United States Basketball Writers Associa-
    tion)
Second Team All-District 13 (National Association of Basket-
    ball Coaches)
WAC Tournament MVP
WAC Freshman of the Year
Member of WAC All-Newcomer and All-Defensive teams
Second Team, All-WAC

All-Holiday Festival (New York City)
Chevrolet Player of the Game (14 March 1991 against University of Virginia; 16 March 1991 against University of Arizona)
Cougar Classic: MVP
Tied NCAA record of 14 blocked shots in a single game: Eastern Kentucky (shares record with David Robinson, Navy vs. N.C.-Wilmington)
Career high 29 points against Eastern Kentucky
Career high 16 rebounds against Arizona State
NCAA freshman season blocked-shot record: 177 blocked shots (5.21 per game average)
WAC season record for blocked shots: 177
Second highest number of blocked shots in an NCAA career: 177
NCAA tournament record for blocked shots in the first round: 10 (vs. Virginia)
BYU Outstanding Player of the Year: Selected by teammates
Scored in double figures in 24 of 34 games
Nine games in double figures in rebounding
Two games in double figures in blocked shots
Team's leading scorer in 14 games
Team's leading rebounder in 16 games
Led BYU to a 21-13 record
Led team to second-place WAC finish
Led team to WAC tournament championship and NCAA post-season berth

1991–93

Missionary: The Church of Jesus Christ of Latter-day Saints: Sydney, Australia
NBA draft: Selected second overall by the Philadelphia 76ers